THE Real YOU

# THE Real YOU

## Making Sense of Relationships

Vicki L. Barnes

Two Harbors Press
212 3rd Avenue North
Minneapolis, MN 55401

ISBN: 978-1-937928-54-4
LCCN: 2012935218

Distributed by Itasca Books

Limericks by Suzzi Marquis
Cover design by Carl Spady

www.peopleskills4u.com

Printed in the United States of America

# DEDICATION

*To my family:*
*I treasure my relationship with each of you.*
*We are a blessed family to have celebrated all together*
*the seventieth wedding anniversary of my parents—our*
*beloved Honey and Poppa—who adore their children,*
*grandchildren, and great grandchildren.*

# TABLE OF CONTENTS

*In relationships personality rules*
*At home and at work and at school.*
*Within these pages discover*
*There are facts to uncover*
*That will serve all your life as your tools.*

*Personality is a T-shirt you wear*
*Which you might not know is there.*
*Yellow, blue, red, or green,*
*These colors it seems*
*Often determine our daily affairs.*

SUZZI MARQUIS

# ■ INTRODUCTION ■

Relationships. We are born into relationships and will spend the rest of our lives building and breaking them. We find our best self and worst self in relationships. Relationships are often a mystery. Why can we find instant connection with a stranger and yet no common ground with a family member? Making sense of relationships requires that we understand how we lead our own lives, even as we assess how others are leading theirs.

Personality types have been my area of expertise for decades. From teaching self-awareness concepts at the University of California, Irvine, to team building training in Fortune 500 companies, to marriage and family education both nationally and internationally, I know that the most complex part of life is understanding and relating with each other.

Out of my early work with the Myers Briggs Type Indicator (MBTI) and several other personality typing methodologies—some of the many that have been developed for use in clinical, business, and popular formats, and all of which got their origins from Greek thinkers like Hippocrates, followed by Galen who first espoused the theory of personality types—I developed the People Skills Series, which includes the Personality Type Indicator, as a method for discovering your personality type and the types of others. Learning what motivates, what matters, and how each type functions is the first step. Applying what each person needs for effective, affirmative relationships, while gaining practical insights for helping yourself and others reach their healthy potential, is another step in using the People Skills Series. This system connects people with different personality types in various environments through understanding, acceptance, and accommodation. People Skills Series is user-friendly, easy to remember, and is a workable tool for building and making sense of relationships.

The Bible tells us to love one another as God has loved us. My faith in God helps me to work at loving others as He has loved me, and my career experience has proved again and again that love and acceptance are increased when understanding is present. Understanding personality types is a key action step toward loving others.

As an educator and a parent, I realized a need to understand the children in our lives. *The Kid Book . . . Surprising Truths about the People We Call Kids* was written to help adults who deal with children recognize the personality types of children and with this recognition to develop skills to most effectively live in relationship with them.

*THE Real YOU* was written at the request of numerous clients, seminar participants, and students. I was asked, "Please give us a book that tells us how to manage the adult relationships in our lives as well as you guided us to manage the individual personality types of kids."

This book is designed to help you understand your own core personality and to direct you in understanding the personality types of the other people in your life. Using the insights and information you find here, you will be able to approach and interact with these people with a new perspective.

When we learn how different personality types approach the same task in their own distinctive ways, we can begin to see these differences in a new light; no longer do we have to see another's approach as right or wrong—merely different. This opens you to the exciting possibilities of more easily coexisting with someone who previously just annoyed you.

Life is about how you interact and relate situation by situation. Making sense out of your relationships is a process—interaction upon interaction, played out with understanding, compassion, and acceptance.

Let's get started.

In the first section you will find out your core personality type, which includes the good news about your strengths, and the bad news, or areas that need work—blind spots. New insights and information will give you tools to help you manage all relationships more effectively. In the Marriage section you will explore the relationship between you and your spouse or intended spouse. The Family section will help you understand your kids, your parents, and other relatives. The Coworker section focuses on individual coworkers, teams, and leaders. The Friends section will bring insights into friend relationships that have brought joy or distress.

Understanding personality types and managing the differences are truly positive action steps toward making sense out of your relationships. When you have completed this book, you will have tools to increase your potential to make sense of the relationships in your life. The reward of making sense of these relationships is joy—your joy and the joy of those to whom you relate.

*The face in the mirror I see*
*is but a part of the whole that is me.*
*If I dig through the clues*
*of personality rules,*
*the whole then has less mystery.*

# YOU

*Successful Relationships Begin with YOU*

Could you quickly list ten core strengths of your personality and ten weaknesses or blind spots? Do you know what motivates you at your deepest level, what your passion is, or what really matters to you in relationships? Do you know what you need for effective, affirming relationships at home, work, and play? Do you understand and manage yourself well?

Do you have an action plan for relating to others so that your life and your relationships make sense? A successful approach starts with you understanding you, and then moves on to understanding others. Knowing yourself and what you bring to the relationship equation, then knowing what the other person brings (their needs, wants, and motives) is the foundation for successful relationships.

Self-knowledge combined with understanding others is a powerful combination for reducing misunderstanding and conflict. I find many people in my audiences know more about their computers or other technological equipment than they do themselves. There is no app for YOU, but the real-life applications you need to know about you are in this book. Successful relationships start with understanding yourself, and then understanding the core motives of others and learning to speak their personality language.

The content in this book will give you a new approach to managing with greater success all the relationships in your life, including the one with yourself. Some relationships are better than others. Even the good ones can become better. Whether it is someone from work, a relative, mate, or a friend, understanding personality types is the foundational building piece of all relationships. A relationship that is not working may be the reason you are reading this in the first place.

Read on. The more you know about yourself and others, the more skills you will have to finally understand that person who you haven't "gotten" yet. Unfortunately, there is no easy app for them either, but increased understanding is before you.

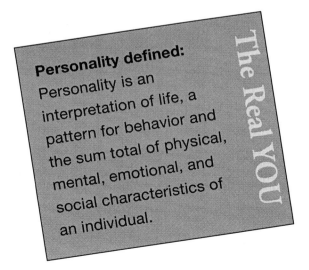

Personality defined:
Personality is an interpretation of life, a pattern for behavior and the sum total of physical, mental, emotional, and social characteristics of an individual.

# CHAPTER 1

# IT'S ALL ABOUT YOU

It truly is about how well you know yourself and manage yourself in all areas of your life. Your thoughts, emotions, and behaviors are the three key aspects of your personality. As you discover your inner potential and create an environment that is conducive to achieving your full potential, you will gain the tools to make sense of some relationships and enrich others. You are the starting place for every relationship.

The Personality Type Assessment on the following pages will give you a point of departure for going on your "making sense of relationships" journey. Take the assessment and score as directed. Do not take this assessment as a spouse, parent, child, employee, or who you'd like to be. Take it as the real you. Think about which words or phrases best describe you most of the time.

Once you have a score at the bottom of each of the four columns, look at your highest score. For each column there will be a group name, a group color, and group symbol. Each of us is unique, yet each of us has a group of core traits that are very similar to the traits of others. It's the similarities we will focus upon.

# PERSONALITY TYPE ASSESSMENT

There are 14 sets of four words or phrases below. Rank the word or phrase in each set GOING ACROSS by assigning: **4** to the word or phrase that **best characterizes, or is most often like you; 3** to the word or phrase that **next best fits you; 2** to the **next best descriptor;** and **1** to the word or phrase that **least describes you.** Use each number only once on the same line. When you have ranked all 14 ACROSS, then add DOWN each column (1 through 14) to get a total for each column.

**EXAMPLE**

| A description of me: | 3 | social | 1 | practical | 4 | decisive | 2 | fair |
|---|---|---|---|---|---|---|---|---|

| A description of me: | | social | | practical | | decisive | | fair |
|---|---|---|---|---|---|---|---|---|
| 1. A description of me: | | cheerful | | purposeful | | forceful | | tactful |
| 2. This group of words best describes me: | | active, enthusiastic, high-spirited, fun, motivator | | serious, intense, honest, logical, wants things right | | decisive, makes things happen, leader | | kind, patient, supportive, easy-going, perceptive |
| 3. I like: | | activities and variety | | structure and order | | accomplishments and winning | | steadiness and balance |
| 4. I am motivated by: | | fun and freedom | | belonging and contributing | | power and results | | peace and harmony |
| 5. When working with a group I: | | want to be with a fun group that doesn't take everything so seriously but gets the work done | | get frustrated with those who make mistakes and are not conscientious | | want to take responsibility for seeing that the group gets it done | | want to be in a group where there's compatibility and cooperation. |

| | | | | |
|---|---|---|---|---|
| 6. A concern is: | boring repetition and same old routines | making mistakes and unpredictability | incompetent people and inefficiency | rushed schedules and work piling up |
| 7. I fear: | loss of relationships | change and disorder | loss of control | loss of my freedom |
| 8. I need: | recognition and affirmations | to be appreciated for my quality work | respect for my achievements | acceptance for who I am not what I do |
| 9. Under stress I can become: | fragmented and disorganized | moody and withdrawn | dictatorial and assertive | overwhelmed and exhausted |
| 10. A motto I relate to: | Think positive. | Plan ahead. | Make a difference. | Be fair and genuine. |
| 11. Areas I need to work on: | interrupting | being critical | being impatient | being indecisive |
| 12. The group of words that best describe my strengths: | inventive, intuitive, optimistic, energetic, encouraging | dependable, thoughtful, organized, integrity, honest | leadership, decisive, perseverance, visionary, drive | diplomatic, compassionate, contented, clarity, neutral |
| 13. I can be: | persuasive | diligent | competitive | accommodating |
| 14. People who know me might use this description: | charismatic, full of ideas, with lots going on, loves people | dependable, organized, practical, does things correctly | self-directed, in charge, determined, accomplishes a great deal | diplomatic, peacemaker, balanced, good listener |
| ADD DOWN each column for the TOTAL | TOTAL___ | TOTAL___ | TOTAL___ | TOTAL___ |

Please turn to the next page to begin to learn about your core personality type.

Why a group name? Names are a way to identify, distinguish, and signify the uniqueness about us. Each name will describe and identify the personality type as a group. Why colors? Using colors with their various shades and hues helps us to see the similarities and the differences. Our commonality is one group color, and our individuality is all the shades and hues of that color. No two humans are identical. Within the four personality types there is unique individuality, thus, colors with the myriad of shades and hues. Why symbols? People learn and grasp concepts in different ways. Using symbols is a visual way to present the concept of each personality type.

If your highest score is in Column 1, your personality name is PROMOTER. Your group color is YELLOW, and your group symbol is a SPRING. Why Promoter? The common traits in this group involve the sociability of people. A person in this group is relationship oriented, a people person who loves to encourage, recruit, and network. Promoting people, relationships, fun, and the good life is their mission.

Why yellow for the Promoter color? Yellow is the color our eyes see of the sun and stars, bright and sparkling. This personality type has charisma and tends to light up a room. Yellow is an attention-getting color and this group enjoys attention. Yellow is the color of a big, bright, bold sunflower, and this personality type can seem big, bright, and bold.

Why spring? Springs are flexible, malleable, and accommodate a great deal of movement and stress. Promoters represent flexibility, animation, and resiliency. They take many of the stresses of life in stride.

If you got your highest score in Column 2, your personality name is PLANNER. Your color is BLUE and your symbol is a BOX. Why Planner? The people represented in this group are practical, analytical problem solvers. They are continually looking for the best way to do something. These are the do-it-right people! They plan life and then follow the plan to live their life on schedule.

Why blue? Bodies of water appear blue and are often deep, covering large areas. The people in this group are deeper, more complex people. They represent a large percentage of the population. Blue is an expression that has come to mean sad or moody. Planners experience more of these feelings than other personality groups.

Why a box? Planners like to have a place for everything and everything in its place. So a box provides that place. This group likes boundaries, rules, and guidelines, and a box represents definition, structure, and something measureable.

If you had your highest score in Column 3, your name is PRODUCER. Your color is RED and your symbol is the CHECKMARK. Why Producer? This group lives to achieve and accomplish. "Time is money" and "Make it happen" are two of their favorite life mottoes. This group finds fulfillment in accomplishments. These are our "human doings." Do, do, do, achieve, accomplish, finish first and best are the words of the internal voices playing in the heads of most Producers.

Why red? Studies show that red worn in competitive sports is an intimidating color to an opponent. People in this group are usually competitive and can be intimidating.

Why the checkmark? Producers like to get it done, check it off the list, and move on to the next set of goals and objectives. The checkmark symbolizes completion and accomplishment and that is what Producers are definitely about.

If you got your highest score in Column 4, your name is PEACEKEEPER. Your color is GREEN and your symbol is an OVAL. Why Peacekeeper? The personality types in this group have characteristics and attributes that make them natural diplomats and mediators. They are kind, balanced people who have a strong sense of fair play and acceptance. This group wants "peace at any price." Peacekeepers do not like to "make waves" or "rock the boat" of life. Why green? As we observe nature, there are many shades of green. The trees and the foliage of nature are a feast for the eyes. This green part of nature has a soothing and calming effect on the observer. Most Peacekeepers are a source of calm and harmony in their environments.

Why oval? An oval has no sharp edges or rough sides, so it just rolls along. It is the shape of an egg. Peacekeepers are known as "good eggs" because they don't get their feathers ruffled easily.

In the next chapters of this section each of the four personality types will be discussed in depth. Start with the personality type that was your highest score, then second highest, third, and then lowest. Depending on your scores, you may find yourself identifying with both of your two top scores. If you have even or balanced scores, start with the Peacekeeper type and see if this is the most like you. If not, read about the type of your next highest score. Read about all the types to confirm the one that best captures your traits.

## PERSONALITY TYPE T-SHIRTS

Before you start to read, please study the four T-shirts chart on the following page. I use T-shirts to represent the personality types. The graphic design on each shirt is yet another tool to help you identify your core personality type. After you complete this book, be thinking about which shirt you wear and when. Do you wear a second or third personality shirt sometimes? Also think about your shade or color of your type. How does your second type fit into the picture?

This book is about making sense of relationships at home, work, and play. Understanding personality types is the place to start. Your key success factor for making sense of your relationships is to understand yourself and others.

The Promoter

**PROMOTER**
Fun  Articulate
Charisma  Variety
Freedom  Inventive
Energizer
Relationships

The Planner

**PLANNER**
I. **Dependable**
 • Schedule
 • Order
II. **Accurate**
 • Perfection
 • Data
III. **Serious**
 • Quality
 • Integrity

The Producer

**PRODUCER**
 • **Action**
 • **Dynamic**  • **Leader**
 • **Focus**  • **Power**
 • **Bold**  • **Results**

The Peacekeeper

**PEACEKEEPER**
Balanced – Moderate
Loyal – Steady
Contented – Listener
Reflective – Supportive

## CLOSE SCORES AND COMBINATIONS

When I am training or speaking about the personality types, the number-one question I'm asked is whether a person can be two personality types. My answer is that everyone of course has a second-highest score. But it is up to you to study the types to see how significant or influential the second type is in your life. My true color is orange. I tie on my own People Skills Indicator, the MBTI, the DISC inventory, and any other personality type test I've ever taken. I am a yellow Promoter at fifty percent and a red Producer the other fifty percent. When you mix equal parts yellow and equal parts red, you get bright orange. Just as I was born with an eye color, body type, and bone structure, I was also born figuratively wearing a personality type T-shirt. Which shirt was I born wearing? I know it's the yellow because I make my decisions with my heart and I lead with emotion versus logic. Can I be logical, make my decisions with my head and be task oriented like a Producer? Absolutely. The situation I'm in is the determining factor. If it's a leadership role, I wear the Producer shirt. If it's a party and I'm a guest, you can find me wearing my yellow T-shirt, telling self-effacing stories and encouraging others.

Your scores make you unique and your combinations are your own unique color with different shading and hues than others. We are individuals within a framework.

## NATURAL COMBINATIONS

Promoter/Peacekeeper or vice versa are natural combinations. Producer/Planner or Planner/Producer are also natural combinations. For the Promoter/Peacekeeper combination, the similarities are that they both are emotion based, make their decisions with their hearts, and are relationship oriented. People with these two top scores are about relationships. They have strong people skills and are in tune with the feelings, hopes, and aspirations of others. They are friendly and likable people specialists.

The other natural blend is the one where the two top scores are close in the Planner and Producer columns. Both of these personality types are logic based, task oriented, and make their decisions with their brain. This combination is quite no nonsense. Getting a job done the right way with efficiency and competency is key to this combination. Plans and achievements are core values for Planner/Producer or Producer/Planner. If you need to build a bridge, change a system, or make something happen, call in this personality type combination.

## OTHER COMBINATIONS

Planner/Peacekeeper and vice versa enjoy a balance of both the ability to task as the Planner and have relationship skills as the Peacekeeper. Both types embrace steadiness and dislike change. They are practical and find rules a comfort. They are indirect communicators who try to get their way by asking a lot of questions, expecting that you will understand and follow the questions to where they are trying to go.

Promoter/Producer or Producer/Promoter can task and relate. They are visionaries who are flexible and future oriented. They are direct communicators, usually making statements and telling versus asking questions. This risk-taking combination often makes for innovative, inventive entrepreneurs.

The Promoter brings the people specialization, and the Producer is driven to make it happen. This combination is all about expediency. They can wing it, make do with just grabbing whatever is available, and get the job done. From a wine bottle as a rolling pin and a shoe heel as a hammer, this is an out-of-the-box thinking combo.

Promoter/Planner is an infrequent combination. This is an opposite combination and sometimes not a true reflection of the top-two core personality types. Childhood environmental factors can influence scores. For example, when a Promoter child was raised in a Planner household where Planner was the personality type language spoken, and systems and order were valued over spontaneity, then the Promoter child desiring to fit in might learn to put the Planner shirt over his or her Promoter shirt. If this is the case, it will be reflected in the scores. Read the whole book and see if you are truly a Promoter/Planner or

Planner/Promoter combination. If so, you have many gifts and talents. You should be able to get along while getting it done right! Producer/Peacekeeper and vice versa is another opposite. The Producer wants to lead and the Peacekeeper wants to walk an independent walk. Peacekeepers don't want to control or be controlled by anyone. Producers like being in charge and enjoy leadership. If these are your top-two scores and they are close, make sure this is your true score. Look at your family of origin. What are/were the personality types of your parents? What personality type language was spoken in your home? Is your job or marriage influencing your scores? If you are truly a rare Producer/Peacekeeper or Peacekeeper/Producer, you will be a well-liked leader who can get it done with compassion.

Make sure you know which shirt you wear first—that's closest to your heart. Knowing yourself in this new way, you are ready to relate to others and meet the needs of their personality types. Often to relate in the best possible way, we need to wear the shirt of another type over our core shirt. As a parent I need to wear the green Peacekeeper shirt over the top of my Promoter shirt. As a person who works as a consultant in corporations and non-profits, I need my red Producer shirt often. I've learned to wear the blue Planner shirt when I travel because you better have it all together in this post-9/11 era.

This book teaches you to know your personality core and to know the personality core of the people in your life. With this knowledge you can figure out what is the right T-shirt to wear to meet the needs of each person with whom you interact. As you travel through life, carry all four shirts in your backpack, briefcase, tote, or purse. You never know when you will need to put on another personality type shirt over your core shirt so you can understand, relate, and speak the language of another personality type. The ability to understand and speak other people's personality type language is a key action step that creates an environment for successful relationships.

CHAPTER 2

# WHAT'S YOUR PERSONALITY TYPE?

## PROMOTERS/YELLOW/SPRING

### PERSONALITY CHARACTERISTICS

Promoters are charismatic people who are able to recruit and enlist the help of others. Their enthusiasm is contagious, and they are Pied Pipers by nature. Getting people to join in is one of their specialties. Promoters are people persons who use personal charm and strong social skills to influence their world. These spirited people are adept at fitting in with those around them. Socially sensitive Promoters prefer to be around others. Youthful in manner, joking, and playful, this yellow Promoter group often has wild personal stories to tell. Articulate and entertaining, they enjoy an audience and the spotlight. With a positive focus and a natural liveliness, they generate energy, excitement, and motivation in others.

Promoters are very intuitive people. They know because they know. Don't ask them how they know because they will just say it's a "gut hunch." These yellow Promoter types have a sixth sense about them. They read people well. Most yellow Promoters are good at understanding body language and nonverbal communication.

Recently, on the way home from a dinner party, I told my husband that one of our favorite young couples was finally pregnant after years of attempting to become pregnant. He said, "Where was I when they made the announcement?" "Oh, they didn't announce it yet," I explained. He then gave me the I-want-to-argue-with-you look. But he knew our history proves I've been right too many times to argue. "So would you mind telling what you saw that I missed?" he requested. "It's the new way Scott watched Kim that tipped me off. He was suddenly her personal bodyguard. She was suddenly breakable, and if he watched her every minute then she wouldn't break."

A month later we received a phone call from Scott and Kim announcing their pregnancy. My husband hung up and asked, "Can I learn the intuitive thing from you?"

It is no accident that Promoters are relationship oriented. This yellow Promoter group makes their decisions with their hearts. The first filter for a decision is asking how this will affect people's values and needs. Putting people first is a natural for this encouraging, social, heart-filled type.

Promoters are adept at building alliances and using relationships to accomplish work. My Promoter friend, Todd, bought a fixer-upper house. All his friends thought he'd never follow through and get his house finished. Todd said, "Oh, just watch. It will be finished sooner than you think. Todd used the Huckleberry Finn/Tom Sawyer method. He had work parties and made them so much fun, a person didn't want to miss any.

It seemed everyone worked hard on the house, except Todd. He raced around keeping everyone in food and drink, while popping hysterical jokes. Todd's friends finished his house in record time.

Spontaneity and fast-paced, decisive action are qualities of this yellow Promoter group. Starting projects and events are their specialty. They also enjoy the finish—especially if there is a celebration. But they often get bogged down in the middle.

Because they love life to be action packed, they live in fear of dull moments, boring people, and slow-paced anything. Being on the cutting edge of events, happenings, and trends is essential to them. These spontaneous, high-energy people are quick paced and animated. Life must be an exciting adventure filled with inspiration, unlimited possibilities, and fun people.

When Promoters are bored or stressed, their verbal behavior intensifies, and they may tend to exaggerate for effect in their stories, talk too much, or interrupt. They become fragmented, ambivalent, and disorganized.

## NEEDS

### Relationships

Promoters truly love people, so it should be expected that relationships are given a high priority in their lives. Because they have smiles on their faces and find conversation easy, they have the uncanny ability to put almost anyone at ease. Promoters are great storytellers and can hold the attention of an audience, be it large or small. They are encouragers par excellence, from motivating the disheartened to intuitively coming alongside to support people and their aspirations.

Yellow Promoters are the cheerleaders of life. Most have good people skills. Their quick wit, charisma, command of language, and ability to laugh at themselves are traits that enhance both their personal and business relationships. Skilled as relationship builders, these are people who care. People seem to sense that Promoters provide a safe place to share their hearts.

I sometimes travel with another Promoter speaker named Kathie. Her shade of yellow is the brightest there is. She can have someone tell her a life story in an airport bathroom while she washes her hands and puts on lipstick. On the plane she makes two new friends before takeoff and three more during the flight.

When I travel with Kathie, I wear my Planner shirt. I become the serious one. Often I sleep on planes. While I sleep, these people tell her incredible secrets about their lives. On the drive from the airport to home, she shares their stories with me.

I always say, "You learned all those stories on a two-hour flight. I can't imagine what would happen on a transatlantic flight."

## Popularity

The Promoter group enjoys liking, but they also have a high need to be liked. Popularity generally comes to them partly because of their cheerful dispositions and caring attitudes. This yellow Promoter group knows the power of the concept: *So, there you are*—here I am. Finding out what others need, and seeing they get it, adds to their popularity.

Their self-effacing humor and willingness to "tell all" about their lives, and "hear all" about yours, makes them easy to be around. Promoters know no strangers. Making friends quickly is easy for them. Many yellow Promoters have a "New Best Friend Syndrome."

Being a bright, taxicab-yellow Promoter, I collect friends in supermarket lines and restaurant bathrooms. Anyone I'm with for over five minutes has the potential of becoming my "new best friend." For our fifth anniversary my husband gave us a weekend at a time management seminar. He didn't need a time management seminar, but he knew if he didn't go with me I'd skip the seminar and go shopping. During the training it became abundantly clear that managing all the plethora of friendships in my life was consuming most of my time. At the end of the weekend we had to summarize and share our action steps. I had one—go home and dump my best friends. The audience gave a collective gasp. My husband said in his nonchalant style, "Don't worry. She has 365, one for every day of the year. She'll make new ones."

## Recognition

Promoters need recognition for their accomplishments. They thrive on positive affirmations and like to see facial expressions and body language that express approval. Don't be stingy with words of appreciation, as it is extremely discouraging for a Promoter to be deprived of positive feedback. For most of this group, encouraging words are food for the soul.

They spend much of their time pumping up others. They really do need to see the inflation process happening and receive feedback that they have made a difference. Promoters will hang in with you and your problems as long as you affirm them and show some progress toward getting it together and working toward living victoriously. Without progress and feedback, color them gone.

Being the eternal optimists, Promoters are cheerleaders of life. If you think you can, you can. They believe victorious living is theirs. Positive Mental Attitude (PMA) is a Promoter way of viewing life. Yellow Promoters particularly dislike criticism for themselves and others. Often they respond to criticism with verbal attacks.

## Variety

Repetition and details have a tough time holding the interest of a Promoter. They need things to be fresh, new, and exciting. Starts are a specialty, and because their enthusiasm spills over onto others, many jump on the bandwagon with them. However, once the newness and initial excitement wears off and repetition starts to set in, Promoters tend to lose interest. Finishes and follow through may be difficult for that reason.

Multitasking is easy and enjoyable for this group. They like to juggle a lot of balls at a time. It is the thrill of the hunt. Can they make it? Risk and a sense of adventure are important. When Promoters become stressed or excited, they tend to talk more and often turn their voice volume to high.

## Flexibility

Their openness to new ideas makes them ready to spring into action at a moment's notice. Promoters like to keep their options open. They are spontaneous and almost never have a problem changing plans midstream. They are not restricted by time constraints and are often poor time managers. Promoters struggle with being on time and having all the supplies needed to complete the task. This flexible group tends to misplace things. Don't give them the original of anything. They don't want that much responsibility. Even though they are creative themselves, they do not find it difficult to get charged up about an idea that was not their own. They will even promote the idea and, like the Pied Pipers they are, will have people lined up behind them. These charismatic leaders attract followers.

## Attention

Whoever said, "All of life is a stage," must have been a Promoter. This yellow group always has a story to tell and the more listeners the better. I had a client who was in the professional placement industry. The company had inside salespeople cold calling for job openings, and outside salespeople calling on companies to help them fill their employee needs. One of the outside sales-people was Marty, a bright-yellow Promoter.

Marty came flying into the office every few days usually around 2:30 p.m. or 3:00 p.m. She always had a story to tell. There was the story about looking for her car for three hours in the wrong parking structure. Finally she made friends with the security guard who drove her to the right parking structure. Then there was the afternoon she whirled in with this story. While having lunch with one of the vice presidents of her largest account the client choked on a sandwich and she performed the Heimlich Maneuver to save the client.

The minute Marty started to tell one of her stories, everyone stopped dialing and listened to the latest adventure in "Marty's Miniseries." My client, the president of the company, was extremely frustrated with these interruptions. Marty, however, was his best salesperson, and he didn't want to upset her. I observed this event for a couple of weeks. I noticed that 2:30 to 3:00 p.m. was the low production point for the inside sales-people. More milling around and trips to the coffee machines occurred then than any other time during the day. The days when Marty came in the production stopped for ten to fifteen minutes. After she left everyone had talked, socialized a short time, and been energized by Marty and her story. The hour after Marty was in the office was the most productive time all week. What time the company lost while Marty was on center stage was regained and exceeded after Marty left. Promoters are energizing storytellers.

Most Promoters have a flair for bringing out the excitement of life and can sometimes take it too far. Whether real life thespians or just a Promoter gone overboard with a story or action, this personality type has been known to create more drama and special effects than is often necessary for the course of normal everyday life. They can be the dramatic star of their own life and sometimes others' lives if self control is not applied.

## MOTIVES

Motives are the things that drive us. Having fun, particularly fun that is relationship oriented, motivates the lively Promoters. If you listen to this yellow group, you will hear the word *fun* used frequently. Jobs, relationships, or anything in which they are involved must be fun. Life must be fun. This group can always find an excuse to have a party. They love giving surprise parties—often for people who don't like change, unpredictable circumstances, or surprises.

In the workplace, birthdays, engagements, marriages, or babies are always an excuse for Promoters to suggest an event. Promoters are great at getting the ball rolling for the party idea. Often they bog down in the details of the planning and following through, though.

As a young bride I loved having friends over. One Saturday we were having three couples over to celebrate one couple's anniversary. I got so busy decorating the house and table, planning the music, and devising a silly game, I forget to plan the food. When the guests arrived I was at the market, racing down the aisles, throwing instant anything into my cart. The meal was a little unusual, but the conversation was lively and everyone had a great time. If you want fine dining, go to a restaurant. If you want fun and the unexpected, go to a Promoter's house for dinner.

## GOOD NEWS/BAD NEWS

First, the good news. This group is casual and fun. They love having a great time in life and taking others along. They do not "sweat the small stuff," and "close enough" is good enough. People will follow them anywhere. And anywhere is often where they are going. Maps, plans, and directions are filled with too many boring details. This group likes to "wing it" and "shoot from the hip." "Leap and the net will appear" is one motto for these eternal optimists.

Promoters can really get themselves, and often others, into major messes. But the "God is Good Scenario" often seems to cover this casual style. God knows that Promoters are impulsive and don't always plan ahead, so He made them creative, innovative, inducing, inspirational, winsome, and energetic. These attributes get them out of their messes. No matter how disastrous their current mess is, they get through it with the motivating thought of what a great story this is going to make!

Lucille Ball, in her television show, *I Love Lucy,* was a pure portrayal of a Promoting yellow spring. The entire series was based on Lucy's messes and how she extricated herself with the help of dear Ethel, who was a Peacekeeper. Lucy's vivid imagination, desire for adventure, and little attention to details formed the foundation for the show.

This yellow Promoter group is innovative. They are the possibility people with an idea a minute. They are great brainstormers, but are sometimes a little impractical. Often they can't implement their ideas. Many are forgetful and, if they don't write down their inspiration, they will forget. Others are so disorganized that even if they write it down they can't find it. Thus, a great concept dies.

Being caring supporters of people, they are generous and willing to share solutions and materials. Many a Promoter has said, "Oh, I have just the book for you." The problem is they don't always follow through, and you don't get the promised help.

What do you think other personality types say about Promoters? The good news is they are fun, funny, tell great stories, usually know a joke or two, and are very friendly and upbeat. They are enjoyable to hang out with because they know how to turn a dull moment into a good time. They have lots of friends, and life around them is exciting, eventful, and energetic.

The bad news is they can be attention-grabbing, obnoxious, interrupting, and conversation dominators. People who work with them talk about their lack of time management skills, flakiness, and undependability. Others say that they are often scattered and impulsive. They can get you into some real messes with their lack of attention to details.

I had a highway patrolman attend two of my personality type seminars. He raised his hand in the second seminar and told the group that he was a Promoter and after the first class he'd done a survey. He said he started noticing the personality types of people who ran out of gas. He stated the Promoters were big offenders because they didn't pay attention to details such as where the gas gauge was pointing.

Some of the most interesting terms I've heard people use when referring to Promoters are: scatter-riffic, out-theres, chaos-causers, clutter-creators, space cadets, larger-than-lifers, pieces of work, con artists, perpetual motion machines, and HD for high drama.

# KEYWORDS THAT DESCRIBE PROMOTERS

| Good News | Bad News |
| --- | --- |
| Articulate | Talkative |
| Charismatic | Superficial |
| Confident | Self-doubting |
| Encouraging | Fawning |
| Gregarious | Obnoxious |
| Persuasive | Overbearing |
| Playful | Childish |
| Optimistic | Unrealistic |
| Positive | Opinionated |
| Fun-Loving | Foolish |
| Brainstorming | Forgetful |
| Innovative | Disorganized |
| Flexible | Undisciplined |
| Inspiring | Unlistening |
| Adaptable | Uncommitted |
| Spontaneous | Impulsive |
| Socially skillful | Melodramatic |
| Friendly | Too trusting |
| Cooperative | Inconsistent |

## MAJOR KEY CHARACTERISTICS

| Personality Type | Promoter |
| --- | --- |
| Roles | Motivator |
| Motives | Have fun, encourage people |
| Needs | Attention, applause, recognition |
| Wants | Relationships, freedom |
| Strengths | Brainstorming, encouraging, enthusiastic, charismatic, creative, articulate, optimistic |
| Limitations | Disorganized, careless, impulsive, unrealistic, obnoxious |
| Focus on . . . | Possibilities and relationships |
| Adept at . . . | Understanding the aspirations of people |
| Ability to . . . | Recruit and enlist |
| Communication:<br>Tells = Direct<br>Asks = Indirect | Direct, energetic, enthusiastic, tells stories, loud, interrupts |
| Likes environment to be . . . | Stimulating, fast-paced, congenial |
| Pluses about any job | The start, the challenge |
| Decisions are . . . | Spontaneous—from the heart |
| Fears | Boredom, being left out, unpopularity |
| When stressed | Loud, obnoxious, impulsive, does shocking attention-getting things |
| Compatible people | People who are possibilities oriented, people oriented, have heart, enjoy life |
| Good at . . . | Recruiting, enlisting, innovation, relationships, selling, encouraging/inspiring others |

# PLANNERS/BLUE/BOX

## PERSONALITY CHARACTERISTICS

Planners like orderly systems. They prefer all information in writing supported by charts and graphs. Planners like outlines. The following in outline form are the major characteristics of Planner personality types: I. PERSONAL, II. WORK, and III. SOCIAL.

### MAJOR CHARACTERISTICS OF PLANNERS

**I. PERSONAL**
   a. Caring
   b. Conforming
   c. Conscientious
   d. Conservative
   e. Creative
   f. Intimate
   g. Honest
      1. High moral standards
      2. Sincere
      3. Has integrity
      4. Guardian of truth
   h. Loyal
   i. Perfectionistic
   j. Self-sacrificing
   k. Sensible
   l. Sensitive
   m. Serious
   n. Sincere
   o. Thinking
   p. Thoughtful
   q. Traditional

**II. WORK**
   a. Accurate
   b. Analytical
   c. Careful
   d. Cautious
   e. Deliberate
   f. Dependable
   g. Detail oriented
   h. Diligent
   i. Disciplined
   j. Dutiful
   k. Finisher
   l. List maker
   m. Hardworking
   n. Neat
   o. No nonsense
   p. Organized
   q. Orderly
   r. Persistent
   s. Planner
   t. Problem solver
   u. Punctual
   v. Quality oriented
   w. Scheduled
   x. Systematic

**III. SOCIAL**
   a. Compassionate
   b. Devoted
   c. Faithful
   d. Idealistic
   e. Realistic
   f. Respectful
   g. Self-sacrificing
   h. Sympathetic
   i. Unobtrusive

## PLANNERS WANT . . .

### Affiliation

Planners are motivated by belonging and serving. They have a strong need for intimacy and affiliation with groups from the family unit to outside organizations. Planners are "joiners." Of special interest to them are service organizations, clubs that support charitable causes, as well as groups that uphold traditions and institutions. Scouting, veteran programs, politics, museums, libraries, church, and the family unit are listed among the Planner's favorites.

They need to be needed. They desire to serve and do their part. Planners are more comfortable as givers than receivers. They are selfless individuals. Find a service award program, and you'll find a Planner who founded it, a Planner who perpetuated it, and a Planner who won the award.

### Honesty

Honesty is a hallmark of the Planner. These are usually the most moral, upright, honest, and sincere among us. They believe that everything should be done with integrity. This code of ethics guides most Planners in all of their decisions from business to social. Their word is their bond.

### Quality

Quality in character, work, and leisure is important to Planners. The desire for perfection is strong in most of them. A favorite quote is, "A job worth doing is worth doing well." Traits like dependable, detail oriented, serious, hardworking, deliberate, and thorough describe most Planners. They are known for the quality they bring to jobs, events, committees, teams, friendships, and families. Phrases like "Foundation of the Organization" and "Rock of Gibraltar" accurately describe these solid citizens.

Planners are deep people. Their strong desire to belong and serve, combined with their desire for perfection, makes them unique. At times they are not easily understood and can be perceived as critical and "nitpickers." As a rule, the other personality types do not have this perfectionist tendency.

## Systems and Order

Planners like to play it safe. They want life to be predictable. That is why it is the Planners who write the rules, draw the maps, design the floor plans, and institute the procedure manuals. Planners must have a plan! "Make the plan and work the plan" is a slogan dear to the heart of a Planner. "A place for everything and everything in its place" is also sweet music to the ears of a Planner.

Planners place heavy emphasis on accuracy and objectivity. They make their decisions with their heads, trying to remain as unemotional as possible. They rely on data to solve problems. "The facts, man, just the facts," is a favor expression for Planners. They tend to be persistent in their analysis, maintaining a critical focus throughout the work or project. In a working environment they like order and clear guidelines. As workers they are independent, follow-through on tasks, and do well at technical jobs.

Planners like to take things one step at a time. These people move down the "yellow brick road" of life one brick at a time. They gather their information through their five senses. They know when they know something because they can see it, hear it, touch it, taste it, or smell it. This process of information gathering makes them very practical people. They are list makers who keep track of important dates like birthdays and anniversaries. Hallmark should get down on company knees and kiss the feet of these card-sending Planners.

## Predictability

Change is not a favorite concept for Planners. Moves, job changes, and changing relationships can become near crisis situations. Status quo suits the ordered life of the Planner.

They are not fond of impromptu and go-with-the-flow situations. Flowing is just too spontaneous. Most Planners believe they can be spontaneous if given enough time.

Being given a surprise party for most Planners is a nightmare: no personal preplanned agenda and no control because they did not personally organize it. "How much is this costing?" and "Where are the receipts?" are just a few of the questions darting in and out of their brains . . . not to mention some of the questionable guests. "Whose invitation list were they on, anyway?"

Under stress, Planners tend to become quiet and continue to seek more information to increase confidence in their knowledge of the situation. This information seeking may hide their avoidance of an issue or their withdrawal from others. It may also delay decision making. Some Planners can fall into the "analysis paralysis" trap.

Because Planners are uncomfortable with emotions, they may try to avoid situations where they have to express emotions. They tend to put quality and accuracy ahead of feelings, even if it might hurt others. The Planner's strong desire for an orderly life causes family members, friends, and fellow workers to say, "Lighten up!," "Just go with the flow!," "Don't rain on my parade!," or "Please show some positive emotions."

One Planner told me the first time someone told him to "Lighten up and go smell the roses," he asked, "How many?"

**Realism**

Planners like things to be real. They paint their pictures with green grass and blue skies. Plants are meant to be real, and they have a difficult time with fake, makeshift, or substitutes. Planners stick with things the way they were meant to be. This group prefers not to wing it or make do. They want the right tool for the job.

This story entitled "Belts Are Supposed to Be Belts" makes the point:

I like to design clothes. Often I find myself mentally picturing an outfit in its completion. Early one fall evening I saw in my head a dramatic black dress. Afraid I'd lose this mental picture, I raced around the house searching for things with which I could simulate the dress. I found an old faded black sheet and a Zorro cape in our costume box. Standing in front of the mirror with the black bedsheet pinned, taped, and hot glued around me, I added the Zorro cape over one shoulder. Peering once more at the outfit in my mind, I noted the belt. It was about an inch wide, made of leather with a roll of silver nail head studs running down the middle. Upon closer scrutiny the belt looked much like a dog collar. Instantly, my mind flashed to the top shelf of my husband's office.

Although our beloved dog, Madchen, had been dead for twelve years, my Planner husband still had the collar. Racing down the hall with Zorro cape flapping, I retrieved the collar. Without breaking stride I tore through the kitchen. Grabbing the ice pick from a drawer, I whirled into the garage. I laid the collar on the workbench, hammered the ice pick through the free end of the collar, and made a hole large enough to poke wire through. Threading the wire through the new hole, I dashed back upstairs to complete the design. Just as I was securing the wire to the buckle on the collar, my husband said, "Well, you are early for a change. Great, I need to make a stop before the dinner party."

In my designing frenzy I had used all the time creating my design, leaving no time to dress for the evening. My decision about what to wear was made when I heard the garage door open and the car's motor start. I would have to hope no one noticed the glue. And I hoped that I remembered to navigate through the pins, keeping the Zorro cape over the belt wiring mess in the back, and that I stayed in dimly lit corners. Throwing on a pair of wonderful earrings in an attempt to tie my creation together, I jumped in the car, faded black bedsheet and all.

I have always operated under the assumption that it's my responsibility to fill all the drive time in the car. After my husband briefed me on who's who of the other dinner guests, he went into his favorite car activity—silence. Reluctantly I participated in this activity for about three minutes. Then I was bored.

I decided it was my turn for my favorite activity, talking. I said, "Did you happen to notice my belt?"

Without removing his eyes from the road or his hands from the wheels, he said, "No." (Planners follow the rules—road signs, speed limits, seat belts buckled, hands on the wheel, and eyes on the road at all times.)

"Just take a quick glance over here because I want to tell you about it," I requested.

"Now, Vicki, you know I'm driving and can't take my eyes off the road," he stated.

"Walk on the wild side," I challenged.

He jerked his head my way in what I guess constituted a glance.

"Well, did you notice anything familiar?" I questioned.

"No, what is supposed to be familiar about your belt?" he asked suspiciously.

"I have on Madchen's old dog collar."

"Vicki, what if we are in an accident and the paramedic notices you're wearing a dog collar for a belt?" he asked mortified.

"Fred, if we are in a terrible accident, the fact that I'm wearing a dog collar for a belt will be the least of my problems." That said, I laughed.

Some personality types can "wing it and make do," and others cannot. Planners like humans to wear belts, and dogs to wear collars.

## Tradition

Planners are very traditional. Holiday traditions are important. They don't want you changing the dressing and gravy recipe from the traditional recipe. Don't throw out all the old ornaments and get a new theme. And, please, put the tree in the same location where it has always been is the request of most Planners.

They plan, ponder, and think about the things that become traditions. Traditions become rules. They like rules and conforming. This desire to do the right thing applies in the wardrobe area also. Of all the personality types, Planners are the ones who appreciate dress codes the most. Jobs that require wearing a uniform are agreeable for Planners. Their need for order gives then an understanding of concepts like standardization, compliance, and uniformity. Planners are generally no-nonsense, no-frills people. Uniforms are practical, hassle free, and economical, especially if the company provides them. All this adds up to a big plus for sensible Planners.

Creative in many areas, their desire to conform and be appropriate overrides any desire to use their creativity in the way they dress. Planners are concerned about the correct attire for each occasion. Being inappropriately dressed to a Planner would be rule-breaking and nonconforming, neither of which is acceptable. Most Planners are too conservative to add their own creative touch to an outfit. Often it is difficult for Planners to change the buttons or add a different belt. They stick to the way the manufacturer designed it. This is also the group that does not rip tags off of pillows and mattresses.

## Conservatism

Conservative by nature, Planners purchase in a low-profile manner. Quality and price are important criteria for Planners. Most would rather have a few good things than a bunch of inexpensive choices. In clothes, they buy natural fabrics, straight-lined, traditionally styled garments that have been deemed always acceptable and appropriate. They generally like conservative colors, patterns, and styles. They select clothes that are basic, durable, and practical. Old standbys and tried-and-true garments appeal to this logical dresser. They enjoy sporty, preppie, and classic designs in their clothing. Twills, Oxford cloth, tweeds, gabardines, and cottons are favorite fabrics for this group. Blazers with leather patches on the elbow, a button-collar shirt, and a pleated skirt complete with loafers paints a classic traditional picture. No fads or gimmicks for this group.

## MOTIVES

Internal drivers for Planners are affiliation and belonging. They have a high need to belong, which includes emotional closeness or intimacy. This blue Planner group seems to be a contradiction.

They desire emotional closeness but also want everything to be right or as close to perfect as possible, and emotional closeness is often less than perfect. They move toward intimacy with high expectation. When their expectations are unmet, they retreat into isolation and lose what motivates them the most, intimacy and connecting.

Another strong motivator for this blue Planner group is contributing to the organizations with which they are affiliated. Here comes another contradiction. Planners want to contribute, and they know the "best way" to do something. If they feel that others are doing it wrong, the Planner group sometimes becomes intolerant and critical, thereby alienating people. Then contributing is a negative experience, and the sense of belonging is lost.

Planners seem to be able to keep track of friends better than any other personality type. They still communicate with grade school friends because they are organized and keep good address records. Planners seem to be the backbones of the class reunion committees. In this ability to keep track of relationships, we see the motive of belonging and connecting come into play.

## GOOD NEWS/BAD NEWS

First, the good news. Planners really want to do things right. In business they discovered the "Best Practices" concepts. In life, if you want to know the most efficient way and often the cheapest way to do something, ask a Planner. Planners give a great deal of thought to the right way to do things. Then they can execute the plan, continually tweaking it for optimum effectiveness. Many in this blue Planner group admit to being perfectionists. Doing it the right way is important to them.

Dependable, conscientious people are found in the blue Planner group. These people are dutiful and diligent. Driven by their high need to serve, they are constantly worried that they didn't do their part. This group is the working backbone of most organizations. Others can and do count on Planners.

Planners like to problem-solve. It is a natural trait they possess. They are detail oriented and thorough. Also, being very realistic, they tend to see the "down side" or the "what can go wrong side." Planners are quality oriented problem solvers. But, how many problems can a person solve in one day? The bad news is this group gets "used" to the advantage of others. Others know that Planners are afraid things will not get done or will fall through the cracks, so they count on these Planners and "dump" more responsibility on them. Blue Planners usually pick up the pieces and fix the mess but not without resentment and grumbling. My Planner friend, Carla, says that if she could pick a new personality color, she would pick yellow. She's tired of being the dependable one while her Promoter husband has all the fun.

The blue Planner group is the only group that wants things perfect. The yellow Promoter group says, "Close enough—let's not make this boring." The red Producer group says, "Do it my way, and get the job done now!," and the green Peacekeeper group says, "Do it the easy way, but don't leave anyone out or hurt anyone's feelings." So the blue Planner group is alone in the perfectionist boat. And none of the other groups understand their compulsion to get it right.

Because the Planners are so realistic and think things all the way through, they tend to be perceived as "rainers on parades," or "carriers of doom and gloom."

Often this group goes unappreciated. Then they become moody, depressed, withdrawn, and critical of others. Then everyone forgets all the great things the Planners accomplished.

Planners, here's something to ponder. As long as the rest of the personality types create "mess ups," Planners will have problems to solve and will always feel needed and valued. So the question would be: Is it good news or bad news that the other three personality types are not prone to perfectionism?

# KEY WORDS THAT DESCRIBE PLANNERS

| Good News | Bad News |
|---|---|
| Precise | Critical |
| Dependable | Obsessive |
| Steadfast | Stubborn |
| Systematic | Rigid |
| Cautious | Suspicious |
| Conscientious | Risk averse |
| Thorough | Excessive |
| Factual | Data bound |
| Creative | Moody |
| Methodical | Plodding |
| Dutiful | Guilt prone |
| Detailed | Nitpicky |
| Perfectionistic | Intense |
| Analytical | Analysis paralysis |
| Composed | Detached |
| Reserved | Unfriendly |
| Economical | Stingy |
| Realistic | Unimaginative |

## MAJOR KEY CHARACTERISTICS

| Personality Type | Planner |
|---|---|
| Role | Problem solver |
| Motives | Belonging and contributing |
| Needs | Appreciation, acceptance, order |
| Wants | Accuracy, security |
| Strengths | Integrity, organization, sincerity, reliability, practicality, thoughtfulness, loyalty |
| Limitations | Self-righteousness, perfectionism, worrisome nature, moodiness, critical nature |
| Focus on . . . | Facts, tasks, and quality |
| Adept at . . . | Applying facts and experience |
| Ability to . . . | Plan and problem-solve |
| Communication: Tells = Direct Asks = Indirect | Indirect, detailed, factual, orderly messaging, prefers written communication |
| Likes environment to be | Organized, functional, practical |
| Pluses about the job | The process, developing systems |
| Decisions are . . . | Calculated, considered |
| Fears | Making mistakes, compromising quality/ standards, being misunderstood, dismissed emotionally |
| Stressors | Change, chaos, sloppy workmanship, irresponsibility |
| When stressed | Withdrawn, moody, cold, disengages, indecisive, "analysis paralysis," holds onto old ways/things |
| Compatible people | People who are serious, dependable, intellectual, deep, appreciative |
| Incompatible people | People who are disorganized, insincere, inauthentic, superficial |
| Good at . . . | Taking responsibility, getting things done, figuring out details, punctuality, quality results, care for needy |
| Needs to work on . . . | People skills, patience, forgiveness, lightening up, being less critical, expecting others to be perfect |

# PRODUCERS/RED/CHECKMARK

Producers are bold, results-oriented people. They take a direct approach to life. Producing results, achieving goals, and gaining power are strong motivators for Producers. They believe "time is money," and they like their information and communication to be bottom line and to the point. At no time do they like to have a point belabored. Producers like to "get the show on the road." A general statement, followed by bullets, is their preferred written style.

## PERSONALITY CHARACTERISTICS

Producers are **driven people.** Their drive to accomplish, combined with their desire to appear competent and knowledgeable in everything, is the force behind their behavior. Many Producers are:

- Optimistic and positive
- Resourceful and pragmatic
- Self-directed
- Self-motivated
- Disciplined about achieving goals
- Strong-willed
- Independent
- Self-sufficient
- Relentless pursuers of results
- Competitive
- Workaholics
- Performance addicts

Producers are **task oriented.** The task, the job, the results—from a deadline being met to a building program being completed—these are the priorities of life for a Producer. However, they only produce results in the areas that interest them. They are take-charge people who are decisive and independent. Producers thrive on competition. They enjoy the challenge of a fight and enjoy the *win* even more. They are not afraid to take risks to get what they want.

They would rather make things happen than deal with people. Some Producers have a difficult time with personal relationships because they think of people as pawns to be used in order to complete the tasks. They possess strong leadership skills and have the ability to get people and projects moving forward to get things done. They usually wind up in leadership positions, regardless of the group or committee they are on. One of the reasons for this is because they are such excellent delegators. For the Producer, *doing* is more important than *being*.

**Producers . . .**

- get things done.

- make things happen.

- like to get the show on the road.

- do things their way.

- get bored with anything that is not the big picture.

- need everyone to be competent and capable.

- are not always in tune with people's feelings.

- manage projects better than personal relationships.

- like quick and practical solutions.

- set goals and believe benchmarks are key.

- are efficient and effective with time and materials.

- make work paramount in life.

■ are focused.

Producers are **leaders.** They manage things, projects, committees, teams, groups, and subordinates with efficiency, organization, and determination. They are . . .

■ dynamic.

■ self-confident.

■ decisive.

■ delegating.

■ organized.

■ commanding respect.

■ possibility oriented.

■ strategic.

■ visionary.

Producers are **usually correct** but are not always popular. They have intense personalities that evoke labels such as . . .

■ A Type.

■ mover and shaker.

■ crusader.

■ king of the jungle.

■ dynamo.

■ dominating.

■ aggressive.

■ controlling.

■ human doing.

## PRODUCERS WANT . . .

### Respect

Producers want and command respect. They drive themselves to "go the extra mile" in order to gain respect. They need to be seen as intelligent, knowledgeable, insightful, correct, competent, and skilled problem solvers. Their hot buttons are respect and admiration. Most Producers would choose to receive accolades for their accomplishments rather than for their acts of kindness.

One high-paid executive told me he would rather have respect than be liked. I told him I thought both were possible if he decided that working on his people skills were a priority. The Producer is caught up in being perceived as confident, competent, and correct.

### Competency in Everyone

Producers are sometimes guilty of the "Dumpster Syndrome." At any initial meeting of another person, Producers can make a snap decision about the person based on the following criteria:

- Is this person competent?

- Will this person be a good networking source?

- How can this person benefit my life?

- Can I learn anything from this person?

- Am I impressed with his or her credentials, demeanor, or appearance?

If the Producer counts too many negatives with their personal rating system, the "Dumpster Syndrome" goes into effect. Mentally, the Producer tosses this type of person out of their electronic gadgets, personal information storage, out of their lives, and into a large mental dumpster because they have made the instantaneous decision that this one is not an asset to them. Motivated by the urge "to be done with that," Producers mentally trash people because clutter and excess are ineffective. Many Producers have found themselves digging frantically through their mental dumpster to retrieve someone they were too quick to judge and found they later needed.

If the Producers' personal rating system seems somewhat harsh, remember that they require competency in themselves first, then in everyone else. Producers are their own strongest critics. They judge themselves based on their last accomplishment.

## Leadership

Producers are born leaders who possess the characteristics and attributes needed to lead. They can rise to the occasion and handle the responsibilities that go with leading or being in charge. Their ability to make quick decisions, delegate, and problem solve are invaluable when solutions are needed in a hurry, which makes them good in emergency situations.

Being in charge often means calling the shots, and most Producers are comfortable calling the shots. This red Producer group is, figuratively speaking, broad shouldered. You can find them out in front in most situations, carrying the major part of the responsibility load. They like responsibility and are good at handling challenging situations.

Being self-confident, driven people, they want it done their way and preferably yesterday with speed and efficiency. And if you happen to be able to read a Producer's mind—that is good also.

## Control

Producers read the parliamentary procedures books, study the rules for the game, learn foreign protocol, and know the pecking order at work. They are constantly networking and often take more than they give from their contacts. "Looking out for #1" is something they do well. Producers know "who's on first" and "what's going down." The reason why is not because they are consumed with a quest to gain knowledge for knowledge's sake. It is because the Producer believes knowledge is power.

If Producers know the rules to the game and their opponents don't, it gives them control. And they always want the power, control, or upper hand. Knowing more than anyone else gives them the leading edge. Producers like to be knowledgeable on everything—true walking Wikipedia, or human search engines. They believe "jack of all trades, master of some" is a good place to start.

Through specialized knowledge, along with understanding the dynamics of power and strategy, they continually rise to the top and master the rest. Believing "knowledge is power," "a job well begun is half done," and "proper preparation prevents poor performance" serves them well. For Producers, life is a game, and they are playing to win!

When a Producer is stressed they move from controlling to overbearing and dictatorial. Their need to accomplish causes them to push forward at all costs, giving little attention to details that may lead to mistakes. People and feelings may also be pushed aside. They become even more competitive, compulsive, and controlling when they don't think they are winning at the game of life. Some can use others as traction or climb up their backs to get ahead.

## MOTIVES

Power and results motivate Producers. *Webster's Dictionary* defines power as the "possession of control, authority, or influence over others." In this definition is found the core of the Producer personality. These leaders, with their strong administrative skills, like power in their lives. They want authority positions, in jobs, projects, and activities/events, whether large or small.

On one end of the spectrum are the Producers who use power and influence to accomplish wonderful achievements for many throughout the world. On the extreme other end of the spectrum are Producers who use power to dominate and control their world.

True to their name, Producers, this group is about achieving results. Making it happen and getting it done motivate this group.

## GOOD NEWS/BAD NEWS

Producers have great strengths and strong limitations or blind spots. The reason for such strong characteristics on both the good news side and bad news side is because our strengths taken too far become our weaknesses. For example most Producers have drive. But drive pushed to the extreme becomes obsession, compulsion, and performance addiction.

The good news is this red Producer group is responsible for starting many great organizations, institutions, programs, projects, causes, and events. They see a need and do something about it. These "make it happen" specialists do just that! Producers are pragmatic. Whatever it takes to get the job done they will do.

The bad news is: sometimes in their passion to achieve results and complete a project, they forget certain details or how what is being accomplished is affecting people. Producers are big-picture people who become extremely impatient when progress is deterred.

This group may have originated the saying, "Who do we have to kill to get the job done?" A good news and bad news combination is about being a super human doing versus being a great human being. Some Producers put so much emphasis on the doing side of life they forget to develop the character qualities. The Producers who say, "He who dies with the most toys wins," values achieving. You have to do well and make lots of money to buy the toys. Many Producers enjoyed varying degrees of financial success due to achieving in jobs and careers.

In the book, *We Are Driven,* by Dr. Robert Hemfelt, Dr. Frank Minirth, and Dr. Paul Mier, is this description: "Humans *being* might jot down fifty chores on their things-to-do list, accomplish only four, and still feel satisfied with themselves. Humans *doing* can complete all fifty tasks and then spend the rest of the day wringing their hands, wondering whether they performed well enough, or whether they were too easy on themselves and should have tackled sixty or sixty-five jobs instead of fifty."

# KEY WORDS THAT DESCRIBE PRODUCERS

| Good News | Bad News |
|---|---|
| Strong task skills | Need to work on people skills |
| Decisive | Opinionated |
| Initiating | Controlling |
| Forceful | Abrasive |
| Driven | Impatient |
| Competitive | Arrogant |
| Goal oriented | Demanding |
| Authoritative | Dictatorial |
| Independent | Aloof |
| Pragmatic | Tactless |
| Productive | Hasty |
| Confident | Egotistic |
| Leadership ability | Bossy |
| Persuasive | Argumentative |
| Global | Selfish |
| Enterprising | Opportunistic |
| Focused | Self-absorbed |
| Straightforward | Sarcastic |

## MAJOR KEY CHARACTERISTICS

| Personality Type | Producer |
|---|---|
| Role | Leader |
| Motives | Power and results |
| Needs | Approval, respect, to be right |
| Wants | Control, leadership |
| Strengths | Decisive, doer, confident, competent, driver, visionary, influential |
| Limitations | Domineering, selfish, insensitive, manipulative, arrogant |
| Focus on . . . | Possibilities and tasks |
| Adept at . . . | Developing concepts |
| Ability to . . . | Accomplish and achieve |
| Communication: Tells = Direct Asks = Indirect | Direct, authoritative, logical, bottom line, unemotional |
| Likes environment to be | Efficient, effective, productive |
| Pluses about the job | Accomplishing the task, winning |
| Decisions are . . . | Decisive—from the head |
| Motto | Time is money; do it right the first time. |
| Fears | Loss of control, being seen as wrong or incompetent, loss of respect |
| Stressors | Incompetent people, out of control situations, not producing enough |
| When stressed | Verbally aggressive, domineering, manipulative, assertive, blunt, pushes harder for production |
| Incompatible people | People who are lazy, non-productive, ineffective, incompetent, weak |
| Compatible people | Other performers, make it happen people, self-assured and competent people |
| Good at | Vision, strategies, making things happen, getting things done, delegating, keeping others accountable, handling emergencies |

# PEACEKEEPERS/GREEN/OVAL

**Personality Characteristics**

Peacekeepers are considerate and value warm personal relationships. They have a strong sense of what people are feeling. They have a collaborative, cooperative style and enjoy being part of a team or family. Environments that place a high priority on teamwork suit them best. They are reliable and steady.

Peacekeepers don't want to control. However, they do not want to be controlled either. They enjoy life when everyone is "doing their own thing," especially them. They are independent, private, and reflective. Doing things in their own space and at their own pace suits them just fine. Although most of this group won't state this, many are thinking it, "Please get out of my space and out of my face!" They do not like demands placed on them. They are patient and tolerant with others and want the same in return. This green Peacekeeper group originated the "everything in moderation" concept. They are middle-of-the-road, moderate people who do not see the necessity of getting "all riled up." Life is meant to be lived at a slow pace. When pushed to produce or respond too rapidly this green Peacekeeper group becomes overwhelmed and stubborn.

A strong belief in the value of each person plus the ability to admire and support the accomplishments of others makes Peacekeepers desirable companions. The Peacekeepers' ability to support others often leads them to choose working in helping professions. They have good counseling skills. They are good listeners and clear thinkers but do not give advice unless they are asked.

Even though Peacekeepers lean toward independence, they make wonderful friends and can be valuable contributors to any organization. They are loyal, tactful, and thoughtful. Their easygoing nature makes them adaptable, agreeable people who are willing to please others. This quality makes it easy for them to get along with everyone. Diplomats of the finest order, when caught in the middle, they are able to remain neutral and open with both sides.

Conciliators by nature, Peacekeepers are skilled at negotiating and mediating because of their ability to understand and speak the language of all the personality types. Their balance and desire for right relationships lead them to their most important role of negotiator.

Peacekeepers promote harmony in any organization. They are motivated by peace and do not operate well in an atmosphere where animosity exists. This green Peacekeeper group serves as anchors in the storms of life. They provide the calm in the troubled waters.

## WANTS AND NEEDS

### Acceptance

They accept others as they are and expect others to be accepting of them. Believing all people are created equal, they are known for their fair treatment of others. Kindness is core to them, both to be given and received. They focus on the good in people and situations. At times, their desire for unconditional acceptance makes it difficult for them to make decisions that may alienate one group or another. Their stand on acceptance makes them "Rights Crusaders." They march in parades promoting everything from children to animal rights.

### Respect

Peacekeepers cherish the right of the individual to be an individual, but they need others to affirm that they are worthy. Worthiness to Peacekeepers comes because they are human beings, and human beings should be respected. Respect for who they are, not what they do, is particularly important to this group. Respect for Peacekeepers is about feelings and human worth.

### Peace

Wanting "peace at any price," they strive to avoid conflict and confrontation at all costs. Controversy is a Peacekeeper's nightmare. So to avoid it, they often keep their mouths shut, refraining from voicing objections or opinions. They are content when life is on an even keel and things are running smoothly. However, their desire for peace and harmony is so strong that they are sometimes willing to pay too high a price. They keep quiet or tell people what they want to hear in order to keep the peace. Passively putting up with unreasonable demands is something they need to guard against. This conflict-avoidance mode causes Peacekeepers to have their wants or needs go unmet. Often these unmet needs and wants linger under the surface until they become resentments.

Those who do not understand the Peacekeepers may think they can continue to push these individuals. Their gentle demeanor may fool some, but eventually their stubborn will of iron surfaces. This "get tough" behavior usually comes as a surprise to observers, but once their boundaries are infringed upon, they will usually let you know, in no uncertain terms, that a line has been crossed. Unfortunately, by this time it is probably too late for damage control.

Peacekeeper Tom was married to Helen the Blamer. For twenty-two years he stoically took the blame for everything from the weather to her health. One morning at 4:00 a.m. he went out to walk the dog. The dog returned. Tom never did. The attorneys handled the divorce, and Tom never spoke to Helen again.

## Independence

Satisfied with solo activities such as reading, computer activities, playing a musical instrument, collecting, gardening, and working on hobbies or projects, Peacekeepers avoid "life in the fast lane."

Content to stay quietly in the background, they don't need a lot of things or people in their lives. Most of the time, these private people keep their own thoughts and feelings to themselves. They are content to be alone much of the time in their personal pursuits. Simple pleasures and uncomplicated lives are more to their liking.

## Balance

They are well-rounded individuals who are not prone to extremes, with an uncanny ability to balance work and play. Emotionally they stay pretty much on an even keel. They do not usually experience extreme highs and lows. This part of their make-up enables them to be cool under pressure. Calm, cool, and collected is an accurate way to describe these mellow people. In a working environment they want the work parceled out at a steady pace. Don't dump last-minute rushes and changes on this type if you can help it—piece out the work.

## MOTIVES

The driving force for Peacekeepers is peace, harmony, and balance in life situations and relationships. This group likes to be firmly grounded in life. They do not like life to be a juggling act or a hanging-off-the-cliff experience.

My friend Richard, who owns a restaurant, recently shared with me that he had been offered an outstanding opportunity to increase his business and profits. He asked the investor, "Will this require me to stay in town the month of January instead of resting in Mexico as I do every January? The investor replied in the affirmative, and Richard said, "In that case, I don't want to increase my business or profit." Most Peacekeepers are not driven and keeping balance in life, which supports peace, is their core motive.

## GOOD NEWS/BAD NEWS

First, the good news. Peacekeepers are universal friends. "What's not to like?" seems to be asked about the green Peacekeeper group. Because of their caring hearts and gentle spirits, these people are usually easy to take and require low maintenance. They make their decisions through their hearts, considering the value of each individual. Harmony, balance, and peace are strong motivators in their decision-making process.

They have a high standard for themselves and others. Peace-keepers have high ideals about people and life situations. They are big fans of the human race and the endeavors of people. This green Peacekeeper group contains the eternal optimists when it comes to people. They try to see the hopes and dreams of others. They know how to hang in with people. These are the kindest human beings in the kingdom.

Because Peacekeepers like to avoid conflict, they can learn to have amazing communication and conflict-resolution skills. It is usually after many negative experiences that these creative Peace-keepers decide "there must be a better way." Ironically, therefore, it is their distaste for conflict that pushes them to face conflicts head on (before they become so large that this green group feels overwhelmed by them).

Peacekeepers keep their heads when others about them are los-ing theirs. They can be calm in a crisis or in the general stress of day-to-day life. This status quo crowd prefers living at a slower, steady pace. However, this group is plagued by what I call the "Whelms." If someone pushes the pace lever on their lives too high, they become overwhelmed. If you listen to the language of a Peacekeeper on the fast-paced track, you will hear lots of sighing and the word "overwhelmed" used frequently. This "peace at any price" group does not see an overloaded, fast-paced life as peace-ful. They are patient, easygoing, nonconfrontational people.

The bad news is: because of their high standards, they are easily disillusioned and disappointed in people. The more sto-ic members of this green Peacekeeper group keep their verbal "shoulds" and "oughts" to themselves. However, this silent disap-proval can be poisonous.

Their kindness is often mistaken for weakness. They can be over-trusting and gullible. This can be a reason why some Peace-keepers become the victims of scams and cons. They sometimes hang in when the hopes are gone and the dreams cannot come true. This group takes a long time to give up on others. There is always the hope for them that tomorrow it will be different. Sometimes it is; sometimes it isn't. Some Peacekeepers tend to stay in unhealthy relationships too long. Their ability to tolerate others, coupled with their tendency to avoid conflict, sometimes prevents this green group from receiving what they need in a relationship. They are willing to give and give without receiving for a long time. BUT—remember this, when these Peacekeepers are pushed to their limit, they are capable of walking away from a relationship and not looking back. They are often unwilling to seek counseling or consider reconciliation at this point. Because Peacekeepers don't want to confront, they can be passive resistive and passive aggressive.

My walking friend, Lynn, is a gentle Peacekeeper, and she is married to a controlling man I call Robert the Red. Last Christmas, Robert the Red gave Lynn a cell phone. She was instructed not to call anyone on it but him. The day after Christmas as we were walking along the oceanfront, her cell rang. Retrieving it from her pocket took too long and it went to voice mail. Both of us are quite low-tech so we couldn't figure out how to retrieve the message. Then when she tried to call, the phone showed no service.

Panicked, we raced to one of the remaining pay phones near the pier. Neither of us had any money. But I had my credit card, which she used to respond to the emergency. The emergency was: "Where was the morning newspaper?"

The second emergency dealt with a misplaced shirt, the third involved the location of his car keys, and the fourth was a demand that she cut her walk short and come home. As we continued toward our planned destination, the cell went off for the fifth time. Lynn reached down and removed it from her pocket and without missing a beat, dropped it into the first trash receptacle we passed.

I said, "Lynn, Robert the Red will kill you!"

She said, "No, he won't. He'll cancel this number and buy me another one. That one I'll leave out so Mutt, his beloved dog, can chew it up. The third one I'll let our granddaughter Katie drop in the toilet. By the time he gets me the fourth one, I'll have its demise figured out, too."

I asked, "I guess confronting is out of the question?"

She laughed and said, "Vicki, you of all people should know I'm going to take the line of least resistance. I would rather solve this situation by being passive than active. And believe me; he will wear down sooner than I do. I will win this battle in my own quiet way."

She was right after the third cell, the phones stopped coming. Now she has a phone only her friends know about.

## KEY WORDS THAT DESCRIBE PEACEKEEPERS

| Good News | Bad News |
| --- | --- |
| Balanced | Overwhelmed |
| Accommodating | Lenient |
| Tolerant | Indulgent |
| Patient | Pushover |
| Kind | Sentimental |
| Good Listener | Codependent |
| Easygoing | Complacent |
| Calm | Unenthusiastic |
| Sympathetic | Timid |
| Moderate | Unmotivated |
| Diplomatic | Indecisive |
| Steady | Hesitant |
| Accommodating | Passive resistive |
| Independent | Uninvolved |
| Responsive | Overcommitted |
| Inoffensive | Weak |
| Practical | Avoiding |
| Laid back | Lazy |

# MAJOR KEY CHARACTERISTICS

| Personality Type | Peacekeeper |
|---|---|
| Role | Diplomat |
| Motives | Peace, balance |
| Needs | Acceptance, respect, independence |
| Wants | Stability, contentment, steady pace |
| Strengths | Clarity, listening, diplomacy, kindness, patience, moderation, adaptability, peace loving, tolerant, balanced |
| Limitations | Indecisive, unmotivated, overly sensitive, stubborn, unproductive, overwhelmed, submissive, uninvolved |
| Focus on . . . | Facts and relationships |
| Adept at . . . | Meeting daily concerns of people |
| Ability to . . . | Collaborate and mediate |
| Communication: Tells = Direct Asks = Indirect | Indirect, empathetic, calm and collected, hesitant to speak up, kind |
| Likes environment to be . . . | Friendly, casual, open-door policy |
| Pluses about the job | The involvement, relationships |
| Decisions are . . . | Consultative—from the heart |
| Fears | Major change, personal problems, being alone in overwhelming circumstances |
| Stressors | Fast pace, disharmony, conflict, instability |
| When stressed | Avoids, isolates, denies, is lazy/couch potato, uses distractions from the problem: TV, sleep, manual activities |
| Incompatible people | People who are controlling, pushy, domineering, demanding, loud |
| Compatible people | People who are collaborative and supportive, helpmates for decisions, solution seekers, respectful of who they are, not what they do |
| Good at . . . | Keeping the peace, showing compassion, staying calm, listening, finding balance, faithful friends, gentleness |

# CHAPTER 3

# YOUR OWN
# ACTION PLAN

You have just finished reading the four personality type descriptions. Or you didn't. Perhaps you read yours, and the personality type of the person who is giving you fits at the moment, and skipped the rest. Please read all four. Even if the relationship you focused on is your crazy-making relationship right now, knowing about all four types will help you in every aspect of your life.

Since I am a Promoter/Producer, I naturally value my own opinion, so below are three "need to know" charts and a list. I don't think you can enjoy life fully without knowing your own key success factors. Remember I am a cheerleader of life (Promoter) and I know you have to get along with most of the humanoids most of the time, so I want to help you do it with more competency (Producer). Thus, the "need to know" part of your action plan.

Living in community with others is tricky at best, but knowing where people are coming from helps a bunch. People interaction can be messy. Words are one of the biggest enemies. Communication—that complicated topic about which hundreds of books have been written—is difficult to master. This book has a simple solution. Understand the personality type and communicate with them in their personality language to the best of your ability. Each personality type is like one of four countries, each with its own language. In effect we are speaking four different personality languages and we all think ours is the official one. This is what often evokes the comments, "If everyone was just like me this would be easier." They are not.

So we have a personality differences problem, which leads to communication problems. What we do not know about other personality types limits our ability to communicate and effectively build successful relationships.

When trying to understand and communicate, questions are often more important than answers. My team-building partners and I often talk about the "Big Q." The Big Q is the question that changes everything. John F. Kennedy asked a Big Q: "Ask not what your country can do for you, but what you can do for your country." This advice caused a paradigm shift in the minds of many Americans.

Each personality type has Big Qs. These questions are about everything in life. These are "Need to Know" questions. As you will see below, each personality type is asking different questions. It could be something as generic as building a small community park. Study the way each personality comes at just this one example. It's easy to see why we have a communication and understanding problem. No wonder you have challenging relationships that need understanding for people to interact successfully.

## "NEED TO KNOW" #1 IS ABOUT THE ANSWERS TO THE QUESTIONS.

**Promoters ask . . .**

- What's the buzz about this . . . what are people saying?
- Can we get others to "buy into" this . . . will it be accepted or have consensus?
- Is there an escape clause . . . do we have options?
- Will this promote unity?

- Is this for the greater good of all of us?
- How do we get the message out and get people on board?

**Planners ask . . .**

- What systems are or will be in place . . . how is it going to work?
- Is there history or a precedent . . . has this been done before?
- What are the experts saying?
- What's the sequence . . . can we take it one step at a time?
- What's the timing on this—do we have a deadline?
- Have we thought of every obstacle that could occur?

**Producers ask . . .**

- Who is in charge?
- What other opportunities could come out of this . . . can we duplicate it if it works?
- Is this new and fresh . . . an original idea?
- How fast can we do it?
- What's the bottom line?
- What's in it for people?

**Peacekeepers ask . . .**

- How does this benefit mankind?
- What good will come out of this?
- Is it compassionate?
- Is it fair and just?
- Will it box us in . . . take away our independence?
- What's the pace going to be . . . is this going to be rushed?

*In the Coworker Section is a chart with questions people ask of leadership. This chart will give you even more insights into your personality type.

## "NEED TO KNOW" #2 IS ABOUT ENVIRONMENT.

(Kinds of environments we thrive, or just survive in, or even fail within.)

## ENVIRONMENTS FOR PERSONALITY TYPE

| Type | Thrive | Survive/Fail |
|------|--------|--------------|
| Promoters | Around people | Isolation |
| | Casual environment | Critical/harsh |
| | Flexible schedule | Routine/boring |
| | Inviting/friendly | Rigidity |
| | | |
| Planners | Structured | Haphazard |
| | Factual | Changing |
| | Unemotional | No guidelines |
| | Secure | Incorrect/mistakes |
| | | |
| Producers | Power/in charge | No freedom |
| | Competitive | No leadership |
| | Everyone competent | Powerless |
| | Challenging | No accomplishments |
| | | |
| Peacekeepers | Harmony | Angry |
| | Respectful | Disloyal |
| | Steady pace | Pressure |
| | Compassionate | Ridicule |

## "NEED TO KNOW" #3 IS ABOUT UNDERSTANDING EMOTIONAL NEEDS.

Emotional needs are defined by www.medical-dictionary.the-freedictionary.com as, "A psychologic or mental requirement of intrapsychic origin that usually centers on such basics feelings as love, fear, anger, sorrow, anxiety, frustrations, depression, and involves the understanding empathy and support of one person for another."

## EMOTIONAL NEEDS

| Promoters Need . . . | Planners Need . . . |
|---|---|
| Attention | To be understood |
| Appreciation | Respect |
| Approval | Support |
| Acceptance | Security |
| Affection | Space |
| Affirmation | Silence |
| Inclusion | Appreciation |
| Recognition | Acceptance |
| **Producers Need . . .** | **Peacekeepers Need . . .** |
| Respect | Fairness |
| Worthiness | Harmony |
| Control | Peace |
| Credit for achievement | Sense of identity |
| Loyalty | Sense of self-worth |
| Support | Steady pace |
| Hide insecurities | Stability |
| Challenge | Acceptance |

**General emotional needs every person requires in order to be fulfilled:**

- Love and be loved for and by both children and adults.
- Love self and have positive self-esteem.
- Belong and have a sense of purpose.
- Feel control over life, some degree of freedom, space, and security.

The People Skills Series helps each of us understand our core strengths and blind spots and those of the three other types. It gives us a common format from which to understand our similarities and differences. So the positive action step is to love someone enough to learn a new language for them. You may not ever become totally fluent but you will improve communication and the relationship exponentially. Truly a win/win for the people you care about and for yourself.

**Positive action step:** love someone enough to learn a new personality language for them. You may not ever become totally fluent but you will improve communication and the relationship exponentially.

The Real YOU

*Marriage is a dance meant for two*
*Held together with love as the glue.*
*Though we often discover*
*As we live with another*
*That love needs some help to re-fuel.*

# SECTION II

# MARRIAGE

## *Till Death Do Us Part*

Statistics tell us the divorce rate is fifty percent of all marriages in America. The data does not break down causes into categories or percentages. An Internet check of reasons for divorce will give you a variety of lists in various orders. But listening to the participants in my weekend retreats, training sessions, and speeches I would say the number-one reason for divorce is money problems. The second reason seems to be a combination of infidelity, addictions, and abuse (both verbal and physical). I hear painful stories far too often about these reasons.

Divorce reason number three is less complicated and easier to fix. It's what I refer to as lack of understanding your spouse's personality type. The marriage suffering from this lack dies a slow death from emotional starvation. Thus killing off the "Till death do us part" vow, they took when married.

Reason number three is why I write books, do trainings, and give speeches. This marital problem is solvable. One wife summed it up well as she bravely said to her husband in front of the whole group, "I didn't understand your personality type and didn't know how to meet your needs. I tried to make you just like me. I never spoke your personality language because I didn't know until just now that you had one. I know you didn't understand my type either and to top it off it we are total opposites. And now we have two misunderstood frustrated people fighting to be understood." Then she smiled, kissed him on the cheek, and holding up her handout she said, "But this *Really Getting to Know You Personality Type Exercise* has given me hope, and this is only the first session."

Countless couples have used the personality type concepts presented in this book to avoid becoming a divorce statistic because of reason number three.

They committed to resolve the difference between misunderstanding and being understood. They took the time to intentionally care. They learned what matters, what motivates, and how to understand their spouses' personality type.

Much of the data and concepts in this Marriage Section come from my audiences' sharing with me. Certified People Skills Series trainers, many of whom are in the marriage counseling/coaching field, have added their feedback on using the People Skills Series Personality Type concepts and materials with their clients and congregations. Collecting data from these two groups has been telling and valuable. Proactive marriage coaching, retreats, and series of classes are on the rise. In this era of increasing divorce rates, couples are being intentional about preserving their marriage and family.

## CHAPTER 4

# A FIRM FOUNDATION OR ON THE ROCKS?

I learned the value of being intentional (in gaining more knowledge about the foundation of a marriage) unintentionally. A local church was holding a ten-week course on marriage. The attendees ranged from engaged couples to those that identified themselves as "married forever" couples. The pastor had asked me to do the personality presentation in week two. I decided to attend week one so I'd have a feel for the audience and curriculum. Being in the "married forever" group, I was surprised when I was challenged to think in a new light.

At that first session the pastor introduced several concepts, but this chart got my attention. He had this triangle. His question was—is God at the top of your marriage?

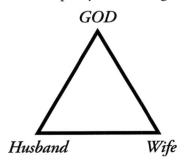

With that question, I did to him what I hope my audiences don't do to me . . . I went on a mental journey as his voice faded into the background. Here's where my journey took me. From the moment I had arrived at the class I started studying the group. My eyes and ears said the marital conditions of some of these couples had some deep needs. I wondered if they needed more help than a ten-week course could provide.

For the rest of the evening and the drive home I kept thinking about some of the couples' dynamics and the triangle. I fell asleep wresting with the triangle.

That night I had this vivid dream. I saw the signage for the retreat, the gathering room. I even saw what I was wearing.

### The Dream

The signage said, "Marriage Enrichment." Thankfully, I was not the Friday night kickoff speaker for this couples retreat. From the moment I arrived late Friday afternoon, my eyes and ears said the marital conditions of some of these couples had much deeper needs. Enrichment would be a temporary Band-Aid, if it would help at all. Certain couples needed more than the program I had planned. The participant notebooks and Power Point presentation I brought were all about enrichment with lots of fun, interactive dialoguing experiences. With a sinking feeling I thought, "How's my material going to work with those couples who weren't making eye contact with each other and barely speaking?" I had three sessions coming up on Saturday. The fact I was stressing was putting it mildly.

During the Friday night opening session I felt like a spy, scrutinizing the audience as they reacted to the speaker. The pastor's main theme was God as the third partner in the marriage. He used a verse from the Bible: "A cord of three strands is not quickly broken." Ecclesiastes 4:12 (NIV).

He had the triangle shown on the previous page as an example. Honestly, I spent more time watching the audience than I did listening to the pastor. But as I was soon to discover, he planted a seed.

After the first night session ended I interacted with as many couples as possible. Finally back in my room, growing more concerned by the minute that my presentation wasn't substantive enough for some in this particular audience, I paced and prayed. Around midnight I grabbed the back of one of my handouts and placed the couples in loosely defined groups based on what I guessed or assessed the condition of their marriage to be. They fell into three categories.

Group one in fact was ready for marriage enrichment. They had energy about them, nudging, patting, and looking into each other eyes. The couples in this group knew how to emotionally cherish each other and it showed. My material was great for them.

Group two, the largest, was in need of many things ranging from the simplest encouragement to the other end of the spectrum, possible professional help. The couples on the low end of the spectrum of group two had frustration and discouragement imprinted on their faces and in their body language. Their lackluster manner silently communicated, "This is hard, we are here acting as if we have it together and hoping and praying we get some help before anyone finds out we are in trouble."

But Group three, although few in number, scared me. I could feel all the hurt, heartbreak, resentment, and anger coming off of these couples. Luckily they were not all sitting in the same area or the air would have been a gray haze of hostility.

Thank heavens it was at this minute I awakened. The dream had been so real, my heart was pounding with anxiety. It took me several minutes to convince myself this was a nightmare and there was no audience waiting in a room to hear me speak. Fortunately, I could not fail because they were dream people not a real audience. Finally I fell back to sleep and the dream continued exactly where I left off.

I dreamed Saturday morning came. Still concerned about how to meet the needs of all three groups, I prayed: "Lord, thank you for giving me this opportunity. The concepts you've given me will strengthen all the couples who signed up for what they needed— enrichment and encouragement. I know from experience that the discouraged will be encouraged and go home with new ways of thinking. Please bless that group mightily. So, Lord, trying to be anxious about nothing as Philippians 4:6 tells me, I'm giving you the other couples who need a lot of baggage unpacked before they can be enriched or encouraged. You made me a personality specialist not a therapist. I'm going with what I have unless you have a better idea quickly. Please guide me to be a blessing to all these couples. Amen"

Stepping up to the microphone and smiling more confidently than I felt, I started to click the remote to bring up my first slide I'd prepared weeks ago for Marriage Enrichment. Suddenly, I found myself turning to the huge white board behind me and quickly drawing two large triangles. This was not in my participants' notebooks or on my Power Point presentation. This is what I drew.

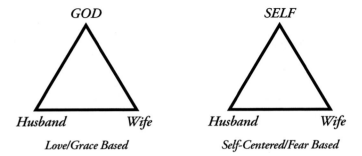

Then I asked, "What does a marriage based on love and grace look like?" The audience started throwing out words and suggestions for what words went where. I noticed the group with the withdrawn body language contributed little. Once Love/Grace Based was complete, I pointed to the Self-Centered/Fear Based triangle and asked what words they would use to describe this marriage. This time I got a few responses from the group I had deemed needed triage, not enrichment. After a short time the group had developed the two triangles on the following page.

As I finished writing the last word on the Self-Centered/Fear Based triangle, I woke again. With a supernatural knowing, I got out of bed, went to my office, grabbed a felt pen and two large pieces of chart paper, and produced the triangles exactly like they had developed in the dream. To this day I believe I got the triangles like they were in the dream.

# Love / Grace Based Marriage
## God

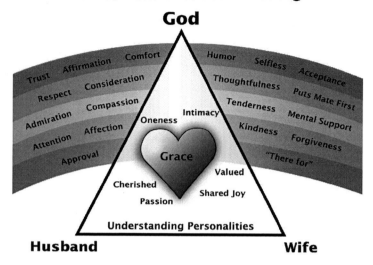

Trust  Affirmation  Comfort  Humor  Selfless  Acceptance

Respect  Consideration  Thoughtfulness  Puts Mate First

Admiration  Compassion  Tenderness  Mental Support

Attention  Affection  Oneness  Intimacy  Kindness  Forgiveness

Approval  Grace  "There for"

Cherished  Valued

Passion  Shared Joy

Understanding Personalities

**Husband**                          **Wife**

# Self-Centered / Fear Based Marriage
## Self

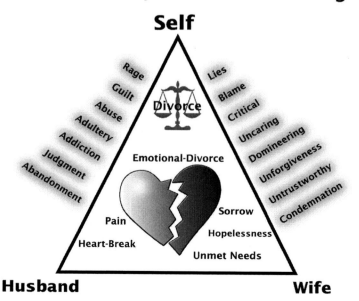

Rage  Lies

Guilt  Blame

Abuse  Divorce  Critical

Adultery  Uncaring  Domineering

Addiction  Emotional-Divorce  Unforgiveness

Judgment  Untrustworthy

Abandonment  Condemnation

Sorrow

Pain  Hopelessness

Heart-Break  Unmet Needs

**Husband**                          **Wife**

The next day I called the pastor and told him about the two triangles. I asked if at my session I could share them with the class. He said yes.

So the next Tuesday evening I did my presentation on personality types in marriage then said, "As you know I'm a Promoter and we always have an amazing story to tell." Launching into my story I built to the point when the two completed triangles would come up on the screen. I did not comment on the content of either triangle. I concluded my session by thanking them for listening and said I'd stay after to answer any questions about any part of my presentation.

People came up and asked the usual questions about opposites attracting and differences in each others' types. Only one woman mentioned the two triangles. She had very sad eyes. In almost a whisper she said, "I have to talk to you about the Self-centered/Fear-based triangle." My heart just ached for her.

I said, "I would love to talk to you but remember I am an expert on personality types and not a therapist."

As it happened, my husband and I attended the next eight classes. We completed the course. At each session I got feedback on the triangles. Throughout the rest of the weeks, there seemed to be a desire on the part of one of the partners, mostly wives, living in the self-centered/fear-based marriages to talk to me about what a revelation this had been. They used terms like "eye opener," "much needed diagnosis," "finally getting honest," an "aha" moment or "the painful sad truth." The fear, sadness, and heartbreak I saw was palpable. I prayed and pleaded with each person who spoke with me about a fear or self-centered marriage to seek professional help.

One of the couples I met in the marriage class asked me to come to their home group and do the personality types and the triangles. I explained that the triangles were not part of my personality materials. The husband said, "I know, but I think there are a few couples in our group who are moving away from love/grace based and in this case I believe a picture or a Power Point would be worth a thousand words."

His impassioned plea, combined with the feedback I received in the ten weeks, made me know that the concept of marriage based on a foundation of love/grace or self-centered/fear was a truth that needed to be faced by every couple. I agreed to go.

Their home group had ten couples. They were refreshingly candid about the triangles. The couples who were solidly anchored on the love/grace foundation had been married less years and had fewer children or were empty nesters who have worked on their marriage. The others by their own admission were still love/grace based, but as one husband stated, "Our foundation is starting to erode. As you know we have four late-in-life kids—two sets of twins, ages five and three. My wife is working part time; I have to travel in my job. We are like two soldiers, each trying to survive one skirmish after another." Then he looked at his wife and said, "Babe, this triangle is going on the fridge. We'll just take it one word or phrase at a time. And, somewhere in this crazy life we are living, our marriage will get back on a firm foundation."

The group cheered. I got teary.

Then the wife of another couple who had admitted that their foundation has gotten a little shaky said, "I want to speak to the couples who have been married fewer years that we have. You don't start out to neglect yourself or your spouse but jobs happen, kids happen, life happens, then the two of you who used to put each other first are now putting each other last. You have become two strangers living in the same house." She paused a moment to blink back tears and said, "Sometimes very angry strangers who once loved each other are now estranged. I watched my parents become angry strangers. They moved from a love/grace-based marriage to self-centered when my dad had an affair. My mother became fearful and eventually they divorced." Looking directly at her husband she said, "I realized as I studied these two charts how easy it is to go from love and grace to the other one. We will not let history repeat itself in our marriage."

The husband stood up and came across the room to hug her. I was crying again.

Over the years I have continued to do couples retreats and workshops about personality types. I always have a segment with the two triangles. These two charts have helped countless couples assess the foundation of their marriage. I share the triangles at every opportunity. The love-based couples use their visual to be encouraged and enriched. Fear-based couples usually remain silent in a group setting. One of the spouses might share with me privately. My role is to listen and recommend professional help.

Recently a husband emailed me after a conference: "Thanks to seeing the two triangles I realized I was the source of fear for my wife and children. I have completed an anger management program and our whole family is in counseling. My family will live on a love/grace-based foundation because God wants it, I want it, and of course my family must have it."

# CHAPTER 5

# YOUR MATE'S PERSONALITY TYPE

As I introduce every marriage session, large or small, I use this quote: "What I do not know about myself and the people I live with limits my ability to build successful relationships." Everyone wants successful relationships. Understanding personality types, starting with yourself, is core in building strong, mutually enriching relationships. As you discovered in the introductory section, there are numerous categories to explore regarding your personality type. You are only responsible for one person's behavior in this marriage. That would be you. You can only change one person in this marriage, still you. The less baggage you bring, the less large objects there will be to trip over. This is a two-person deal but you can only control one, you again.

Bringing a "YOU" into the marriage, one that knows more about yourself than your current technological gadgets or social networking sites, will give the marriage a strong start, or add stability if you are already married. A new understanding of your personality type strengths and blind spots will bring new insights to the marriage that will enhance and enrich your relationship. So part one of a solid marriage is for both partners to first understand who they are.

Now that you have focused on you, let's be intentional about focusing on your mate.

What I do not know about my mate's personality type . . .

- limits my ability to meet his or her emotional needs.

- limits my ability to know what motivates.

- limits my ability to know what matters.

- limits me from building a strong positive relationship.

## MEETING YOUR MATE'S EMOTIONAL NEEDS

As discussed in Chapter 3, everyone has general emotional needs. Then, there are emotional needs related to marriage, and then specific emotional needs based on personality type. There are also wants and desires, but we first focus on the emotional needs specific to the four individual types.

Marital emotional needs, depending on what website or book you read, range from trust, respect, open communication, affection, sex, financial and domestic support, to honesty and admiration, to name some at the top of the lists. If you know and understand your spouse's personality and the emotional needs that come with their personality type, you will be better equipped to meet your mate's marital emotional needs. Those with met needs are more likely to meet the needs of others. This makes a win/win situation and relationship.

On the following page is a chart also found in Chapter 3. This time read it with your significant other in mind.

## MEETING YOUR MATE'S PERSONALITY EMOTIONAL NEEDS

| Promoters Need . . . | Planners Need . . . |
|---|---|
| Attention | To be understood |
| Appreciation | Respect |
| Approval | Support |
| Acceptance | Security |
| Affection | Space |
| Affirmation | Silence |
| Inclusion | Appreciation |
| Recognition | Acceptance |
| Producers Need . . . | Peacekeepers Need . . . |
| Respect | To be understood |
| Worthiness | Harmony |
| Control | Peace |
| Credit for achievement | Sense of identity |
| Loyalty | Sense of self-worth |
| Support | Steady pace |
| Hide insecurities | Stability |
| Challenge | Acceptance |

## KNOWING WHAT MOTIVATES YOUR MATE

| Promoter Motivation | Planner Motivation |
|---|---|
| Fun and people interaction | Belonging and contributing |
| Producer Motivation | Peacekeeper Motivation |
| Power and results | Peace and balance |

## KNOWING WHAT MATTERS TO YOUR MATE

| Promoter | Planner |
|---|---|
| Please others and self | Please others |
| Social life | Order |
| Popularity | Organization |
| Freedom | Schedules |
| Spontaneity | Rules |
| Creativity | Security |
| Variety | Routine |
| Fun | Honesty |
| **Producer** | **Peacekeeper** |
| Please self | Please others |
| Achievement | Independence |
| Accomplishment | No conflict |
| Competency | No confrontation |
| Winning | No pressure |
| To be right | Steady pace |
| Respect | Security |
| Leadership | Kindness |

The more you know about yourself and your mate, the stronger the relationship. It is rarely the similarities that trip us up in a marriage; it's the differences. In the header of each participant manual for my workshops it says, "Managing the differences makes all the difference."

The next charts, when learned and applied like the three before them, will take you a long way down the road toward understanding. Understanding means meeting emotional needs, knowing wants and what matters, and finally, knowing every other aspect of your mate's personality. Understanding is the foundation upon which to build a strong, mutually respectful loving marriage.

# INSIGHTS INTO YOUR MATE'S PERSONALITY

## Yellow Promoter

**Good news:**
They are relational. They lead with their heart. Keep marriage fresh and exciting. Enthusiastic and excited about life. Compromising and forgiving. Fun. Encourager.

**Bad news:**
Starts strong, lacks follow through. Details like finances, records, and schedules are not a priority. Forgetful and often messy. Interrupts. Unreliable. Easily distracted. Late.

**Realize they are:**
Charismatic, social, and need to be popular. Enjoy status. Want to hide insecurities.

**Controls others with:**
Wit, humor, charm, powers of persuasion, persistence, deception, and encouragement.

**Causes of discouragement:**
Future looks hopeless right now, life is not fun, relationship problems, feeling unaccepted and unloved.

**Fears:**
Being unpopular, isolation, getting old, unattractive, being bored and poor.

**Stress releases:**
Going outside self, talking with friends, shopping, eating out, playing or partying.

**Energy levels:**
Highs and low extremes, no middle. Race until they crash and burn.

## INSIGHTS INTO YOUR MATE'S PERSONALITY

| Blue Planner |
| --- |
| **Good news:**<br>They are honest; remember important dates; are committed to celebrating important dates and starting and keeping traditions. Neat, organized, financially responsible, and plan ahead. Loyal, logical, dependable, and sincere. |
| **Bad news:**<br>Critical, perfectionist, moody, and self-righteous. Unforgiving, negative, inflexible, and holds a grudge. Self-focused. Hard to please. Second guesses. Places blame and can engage in guilt tripping. Worrier. |
| **Realize they are:**<br>Quality-seeking solid citizens. Desire intimacy even if they sabotage it with negatives. Going to do it right. Insecure. |
| **Controls others with:**<br>Moodiness, selfishness, negativity, nagging, nitpicking, and anger. |
| **Causes of discouragement:**<br>Life is not perfect. Sense of failure, not measuring up. Struggles with seeing the glass half empty. People who don't do things the logical way. Irresponsible people. Their own negativity. Being misunderstood. Controlled by moods. |
| **Fears:**<br>Making a mistake, being a failure, loss of security, compromising quality, change, and financial setbacks. |
| **Stress releases:**<br>Withdraw into solitary activities such as puzzles, models, collections, read, TV, movie, computer games, studies, or meditation. |
| **Energy levels:**<br>Moderate, drained by disorder and people. |

## INSIGHTS INTO YOUR MATE'S PERSONALITY

| Red Producer |
|---|
| **Good news:**<br>Leader, sees the big picture, optimistic, sets goals and achieves them. Champions people and causes they believe in. Logical, likes change. |
| **Bad news:**<br>Controlling, fears showing what could be perceived as inadequacies. Workaholic, self-confident but not self-loving. Strict, tough, bossy, driven, manipulative, and unfeeling. |
| **Realize they are:**<br>Decisive, driven, problem solvers. Good to have in your corner. |
| **Controls others with:**<br>Their powerful "don't take no" for an answer personality; intimidation/ my way or the highway, guilt, anger, and fear tactics. |
| **Causes of discouragement:**<br>People who don't see it their way. No successes, feeling incompetent, and too much human drama. |
| **Fears:**<br>Loss of control, job, or security. Financial disasters. Relationships they can't control. |
| **Stress releases:**<br>Works harder, grips situation and people tighter. More strategizing and exercise. |
| **Energy levels:**<br>Highest of all types. Driven to excel. |

# INSIGHTS INTO YOUR MATE'S PERSONALITY

| Green Peacekeeper |
|---|
| **Good news:**<br>Relational and emotionally based. Kind, easygoing, balanced, even, and diplomatic. Sensitive to moods of others. Comforting, stays calm, agreeable, and patient. |
| **Bad news:**<br>Indecisive, easily overwhelmed, stubborn, passive resistive, nonconfrontational, low in drive, and little sense of urgency. |
| **Realize they are:**<br>Caring, good listeners, stable, content, fair, and very loving. |
| **Controls others with:**<br>Procrastination, stubbornness, and passivity; inability to cope, withdrawing physically and emotionally. Lack of planning and executing. |
| **Causes of discouragement:**<br>Life is out of harmony and balance. Pressure to produce. Confrontations. Lack of independence. |
| **Fears:**<br>Conflict, change, making decisions fast, loss of security, and angry people. |
| **Stress releases:**<br>Goes into shell, sits on couch stares. Reading, TV, or eating. Solitude and sleep. |
| **Energy levels:**<br>Lowest, needs a slow steady pace without confrontations. |

## MUST KNOW

| Yellow Promoter | Blue Planner |
|---|---|
| 19% of total population | 35% of total population |
| Female 65%—male 35% | Male 60%—female 40% |
| Heart makes decision—emotion based | Brain makes decision—logic based |
| Direct communicator—tells vs. asks | Indirect communicator—asks vs. tells |
| Prefers relationships over tasks | Prefers tasks over relating with others |
| More extroverts than introverts | Close split/extroverts and introverts |
| Seeks change | Avoids change |
| **Red Producer** | **Green Peacekeeper** |
| 14% of total population | 32% of total population |
| Male 60%—female 40% | Female 65%—male 35% |
| Brain makes decision—logic based | Heart makes decision—emotion based |
| Direct communicator—tells vs. asks | Indirect communicator—asks vs. tells |
| Prefers tasks over relating with others | Prefers relationships over tasks |
| More extroverts than introverts | Close split/extroverts and introverts |
| Seeks change | Avoids change |

# CHAPTER 6

# MORE OR LESS ALIKE?

The number-one question I'm asked as I travel around speaking about personality types is, "Do opposites attract when it comes to mates?" My answer comes from three sources: audience feedback, observation, and my own marriage. My answer is, "Often, and if you don't know your mate's personality type it can mean disaster or divorce. We are naturally attracted to those we least understand. We marry them and spend the rest of our lives succeeding or failing to understand them. We are frustrated because they are not like us. Yet, isn't that exactly what we were attracted to in the first place?"

On the next pages you will find a **"Similarities and Differences"** chart for all the personality combinations. The first chart is the Promoter/Planner comparison. If you will notice, there are two similarities and seventeen differences. If you are in this kind of marriage or relationship, a look at the chart should make you laugh or cry, depending on how you are managing the differences.

The stories I hear from this personality type combination are all different, but the topic is the same. This personality partnership "disagrees" and or fights (depending on the maturity level and emotional healthiness of the couples) over systems and order. The Planner wants to "Make a plan and work the plan," and the Promoter is racing through life with no time to get a plan, much less execute it. Promoters will tell you planning is boring and takes the thrill out of life. Planners who hate change go crazy with their Promoter spouse's unstructured and inventive lifestyle. Different or opposite personality types are the ones that challenge us most. It is these differences in personalities that cause conflict and loss of harmony in any relationships. We relate better to our own type and similar types than our total opposites. Some marriage combinations are just more opposite than others. A quick glance at the charts will show you that the two most opposite marriages are Producer/Peacekeeper and the Promoter/Planner.

## SIMILARITIES

People interaction is important;
acceptance and approval from others is of utmost importance.

## DIFFERENCES

| Promoter | Planner |
|---|---|
| Simple personality | Complex personality |
| Playful and casual | Serious and formal |
| High profile | Low profile |
| Large groups | Intimate groups |
| Trusting | Suspicious |
| Innovative | Creative |
| Flexible | Structured |
| Spontaneous | Planned |
| Likes change | Dislikes change |
| Scattered productivity | Systematic productivity |
| Hang loose | Uptight |
| Direct | Indirect |
| Close enough | Precise |
| Generalist | Specialist |
| Possibilities | Practical |
| Relationships | Tasks |
| Feeling | Thinking |

## SIMILARITIES

Relationship oriented, casual style, good natured, patient, welcomes advice, tolerant, accepting, forgiving, nonjudgmental, feeling.

## DIFFERENCES

| Promoter | Peacekeeper |
|---|---|
| Spontaneous | Steady |
| High profile | Low profile |
| Possibilities | Practical |
| Stimulating | Soothing |
| Aggressive | Passive |
| Proactive | Reactive |
| Impulsive | Methodical |
| Emotional | Logical |
| Socialite | Loner |
| Likes change | Dislikes change |

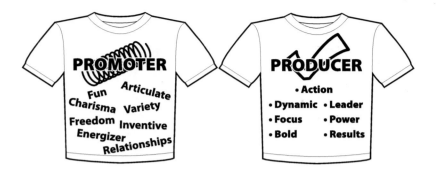

## SIMILARITIES

Strong verbal skills, loves freedom, risk takers, arguments stimulate them, rebellious, nonconforming, possibility oriented, present and future oriented, innovative, inventive, entrepreneurial.

## DIFFERENCES

| Promoter | Producer |
|---|---|
| Relationship oriented | Task oriented |
| Good natured | Impatient |
| Carefree | Intense |
| Nonpossessive | Possessive |
| Scattered productivity | Targeted productivity |
| Accepts advice | Does not want advice |
| Unfocused | Driven |
| Undisciplined | Well disciplined |
| Shares emotions | Does not share emotions |
| Feeling | Thinking |

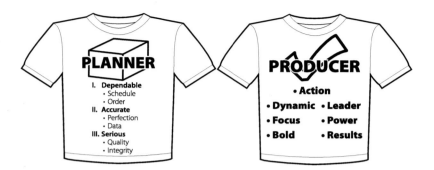

## SIMILARITIES

Achievers, want to be in control, task oriented, determined, responsible, makes decision with head, complex personalities.

## DIFFERENCES

| Planner | Producer |
| --- | --- |
| Detailed | General |
| Specifics | Big picture |
| Dislikes change | Creates change |
| Self-righteous | Arrogant |
| Pessimistic | Optimistic |
| Focused on past | Focused on future |
| Practical | Possibilities |
| Perfectionist | Productivity |
| Indirect | Direct |
| Process | Progress |
| Quality | Quantity |
| Analytical | Logical |

## SIMILARITIES

Practical, steady, compliant with rules, dislikes change.

## DIFFERENCES

| Planner | Peacekeeper |
|---|---|
| Task oriented | Relationship oriented |
| To be good morally | To feel good within |
| Analytical | Solution seeker |
| Intense | Relaxed |
| Focused on past | Focused on present |
| Demanding | Nondemanding |
| Complex personality | Simple personality |
| Formal | Casual |
| Thinking | Feeling |
| Highly structured | Medium to low structure |
| Self-focused | Other focused |
| Self-righteous | Nonjudgmental |
| Needs to belong | Self-contained |
| Likes group process | Solo or very small group |
| Leadership | Independence |

## SIMILARITIES

Independent.

## DIFFERENCES

| Producer | Peacekeeper |
| --- | --- |
| Task oriented | Relationship oriented |
| Controls others | Controls self |
| Pleases self | Pleases others |
| Change | Stability |
| Delegator | Doer |
| Tense | Relaxed |
| Impatient | Patient |
| Demanding | Nondemanding |
| Tactless | Tactful |
| Gives advice | Seeks advice |
| Poor listener | Good listener |
| Possibilities | Practical |
| Thinking | Feeling |
| Multitasking | Single projects |
| Likes lots to do | Overwhelmed by too much |
| Achievement | Enjoying |
| Doing | Being |
| Results | Process |

# CHAPTER 7

# ONE PLUS ONE MAKES A COUPLE

As the T-shirt charts in the last chapter showed, some marriages have more similarities than others. Some combinations are more task oriented and others are more relationship oriented. On the following pages are additional insights and details of the marital combinations.

## PROMOTERS AND PLANNERS

**Pluses:** The Planner provides thoughtfulness and dependability. The Promoter provides energy and fun.

*The Planner provides the perfectly planned beautifully executed picnic and the Promoter brings the fun and sunshine . . . even on a rainy day.*

**Minuses:** Planners can view Promoters as irresponsible and undependable. Promoters can see Planners as boring and critical.

*The Promoter, trying to put some spark in the marriage, writes the Planner a sexy love note. The Planner corrects the spelling and sends it back unanswered.*

## PROMOTER AND PRODUCER

**Pluses:** Both like change and adventure. Each has a direct communication style and likes to make things happen.

*This high adventure couple has their first child. ASAP they toss her in a backpack with her bottles and diapers, strap her in, and keep on hiking the mountains.*

**Minuses:** Being two opinionated, assertive people, both try to inventively get their way.

*Too busy to communicate and seeking the element of surprise, this couple each booked a nonrefundable outdoor adventure vacation on two different continents for the exact same week. P.S. They went on the Producer's vacation. The Promoter enthusiastically gave hers to her sister.*

## PROMOTER AND PEACEKEEPER

**Pluses:** Emotionally based, kindhearted, easygoing, relational, and popular.

*This couple, so busy saying warm, genuinely heartfelt goodbyes to all the friends who had attended their baby shower, drove off with the car seat on top of the car. Thankfully, the grandmother was still sitting on the porch, holding the baby.*

**Minuses:** Organization, planning and routines are not strong attributes for this social couple. No sense of urgency. Very protective of independence and ability to go with the flow.

*One Promoter/Peacekeeper couple joyfully said, "Oh, our friends know they can drop in anytime because they know they will not ruin our plans . . . we never have any. Or if we do, we can usually be flexible."*

## PROMOTER AND PROMOTER

**Pluses:** Fun, exciting, outgoing, carefree, and great to party with.
*I rarely see two Promoters married. The few I've heard about are usually second or third marriages and they seem to gravitate toward Las Vegas chapel weddings and quickie Nevada divorces.*

**Minuses:** Lack of details, records, files, organization, or schedules. All relationships and no tasking for this couple.
*I know one Promoter marriage, a third for both, a painter and a writer. Last time I checked on them he, laughing, said, "Oh, we're having a ball. Of course, we are wanted by both the DMV and the IRS."*

## PLANNER AND PRODUCER

**Pluses:** Organized, determined, focused, planning their future, financially secure or planning how to get there. Logical and task oriented.
*A wedding put on by this couple was about details and impressiveness. The Planner thought of everything and then some. The Producer wanted it to be the best ever, a model for everyone to use in their future weddings.*

**Minuses:** Potential for cold, no-nonsense approach to life and family. Fun, excitement, and joy could be missing.
*An extreme case is two corporate executive parents with three children, eight cars, and more houses than they can visit. The Promoter son said, "I have a trust fund but I sure could use a hug."*

## PLANNER AND PEACEKEEPER

**Pluses:** Both are practical. The Planner brings logic and the ability to task, while the Peacekeeper brings emotional insights and relationship skills.
*I tell my audiences, "If this couple combination invites you to dinner, go, don't miss it. The Planner will serve an exquisitely executed meal and the Peacekeeper will bring the warmth and joy for a lovely evening."*

**Minuses:** Dislike change, neither wants the boat rocked. Could be boring, too quiet and set in their ways. No spontaneity.

*An older couple with plenty of financial security has framed in the entry hall the first dollar they ever made. But to visit their house is a step into the past. It's their original house, complete with mostly early married furniture. The garage is piled to the rafters with things too good to throw away. Their two old clunker cars are practically encased in clutter. They have saved every newspaper for each of their birthdays since they were married fifty-two years ago. Good luck to the children who have to someday to clean out this place.*

## PLANNER AND PLANNER

**Pluses:** Every tiny detail is covered. This is an "i" dotting, "t" crossing couple. Everything is insured, and broken things are quickly fixed perfectly.

*This is not a common marriage but somehow my husband and I have managed to always have two blue Planners as we call them, as across-the-street neighbors. We get to look at perfection daily. Their garage is an icon for their lives. Well-planned quality cupboards and shelving cover the walls, giving a visual for the neighbors of a place for everything and everything in its place.*

*A shiny epoxied floor, with a straight line painted down the exact center. At the high point, the two tennis balls extend from cords attached to the ceiling so that neither driver goes an inch over the line. Our garage, on the other hand, has more of a crammed in, concrete floor with grease stains theme.*

**Minus:** Victims of analysis paralysis. Rigid, rules are rules. Not a glimpse of spontaneity. Fun night is on the calendar for next month. Hate change.

*This Planner couple came up to me at a retreat and said, "We think we could be your poster couple for the Planner/Planner marriage. We live in analysis paralysis. We can afford new TVs, furniture, and cars but we research everything to death, generating stacks of Excel spreadsheets with pros and cons. Then we have so much confusing and conflicting information we just keep what we have."*

*The wife said, "My car finally died and I used my bike and public transportation for six months because I could not decide on what car to buy. Impending winter snow forced me to buy a 4-wheel-drive automobile."*

## PRODUCER AND PEACEKEEPER

**Pluses:** The Producer brings logic, task orientation, vision, goals, and strategies to the marriage and family life. The Peacekeeper brings heart to the marriage. Excellent relationship skills and the ability to be "the voice of reason" in conflict is a vital part of this extremely opposite marital combination. This relationship gets very interesting when the husband is the Peacekeeper and wife is the Producer.

*My model for this relationship is a forty-something couple. She is a lawyer who travels a great deal and he is a stay-at-home parent and freelance sportswriter.*

*Both spouses seem to truly embrace their roles. He shares anecdotes about this role-reversal marriage that make me grin. He said, "Thank heavens I'm a sports nut because that gives me something in common with the other guys in our couples group. But truthfully, sometimes I find myself tuning out the guys and perking up my ears when several of the wives are talking about fabulous one-pan meals and miracle stain removers."*

**Minuses:** Independence is the only thing this couple has in common if you look at the chart for this personality combination. This one commonality can be both good and bad. Producers can be very controlling and Peacekeepers don't want to control or be controlled. Control can be the main problem in this marriage. Often, the Producer is trying to control, manipulate, and dominate the Peacekeeper. The Peacekeeper abhors conflict and seeks freedom to live life on his or her own terms. My way or the highway can be a red Producer expression. So the Producer advances while the Peacekeeper goes silent and retreats into emotional absentness in order to avoid conflict.

*This Peacekeeper wife didn't even have to tell me what was wrong when she came to greet me at the conference I was giving. She was a daughter of a good friend of mine. I knew her when she was in high school. She was popular, a tower of inner strength, and full of compassion. I remember that she saw the need for a clothing program at one of the poorer schools in her town and made it happen. Now she was dull-eyed and slumping. I suggested we meet later, one on one. Her story was familiar. The Producer husband started to try to change her on the honeymoon. He wanted her to get more guts, be bold and adventuresome like him.*

*As soon as they were home his main directives became about leaving her nonprofit job, which was her passion, and getting a job in corporate America that paid better. From his perspective she seemed to do very little right. Quietly she said, "Thank heavens, I haven't been able to get pregnant. I don't want to have a baby in this toxic environment. Plus I don't want to raise a child around someone who has stolen my joy." I had plenty to say on this topic later but at the moment I just pulled her to me and held her like I knew her mother would want me to.*

## PRODUCER AND PRODUCER

**Pluses:** Driven, often financially successful, involved in making a difference by casting visions for charities and community. Powerful, self-confident and strong willed.

*I met this couple twenty years ago at one of my first marriage seminars. Two strikingly handsome young people came up afterward and said, "We are a red/red couple; you didn't say a word about our combinations."*

*Truthfully, I hadn't given much thought to this combination. I figured it would be rare at best. I assumed if they even dated they would self-destruct soon because two forces of nature this strong would have a hard time coexisting. But here they were married four years and according to them doing great. I asked them how they managed the "who was in charge" issue?*

*The husband said, "We both have business backgrounds and while dating we decided to use a team-building model. Whichever one of us has the most skills, experience, or strengths on an issue or task does it and the other tries to trust, not second guess or interfere.*

*With a tender glance at his wife, he said, "Most of the times it works." I have been able to keep track of this couple and they will soon celebrate twenty-five years of marriage at a party put on by their three children.*

**Minuses:** Control issues, married to their jobs, low intimacy with high achievement and accomplishments that often don't nourish the marriage.

*In the last twenty years I still have yet to meet many Producer/ Producer combinations. However, here is a couple in my life right now. Older Producer man marries eighteen years younger rising-star business woman as wife number three. She is confident, extremely capable and a powerhouse Producer. His first wife was a lovely gentle green who felt powerless and incompetent from day one and ran off with another man. Wife number two was as powerful and successful as our groom. He and wife two refined the word ugly during their divorce so I asked him, why another Producer wife? Candidly he said, "I'm retired but I still love the thrill of the business hunt. With this woman I can live it again." It will be interesting to see if this becomes a win/win or a loss of power for one of them.*

## PEACEKEEPER AND PEACEKEEPER

**Pluses:** Kind, stable, content, low pressure, slow-paced free spirits; satisfied with status quo; diplomatic, caring, and gentle. This is a very popular universal donor couple. Great listeners. They know how to stay mutual and neutral with family and friends.

*Here is another marital combination that doesn't occur that often. I met this couple at a singles retreat. They had met in the group and even though now married couldn't leave all the relationships behind so they came as helpers. This was a couple who appeared to be late forties, early fifties. They excitedly told me this was a first marriage for her and a second for him, and they*

*were celebrating their "one slash fifteen anniversary" next month.
I asked what a "one slash fifteen" was.*

*Their faces beamed as the wife said, "One slash fifteen just
confirms everything you've said about Peacekeeper today. One is
for our marriage one year anniversary and fifteen is for the anniversary of the day we met." Before I could ask she answered, "Yes,
we dated for fourteen years before we got married. We are both
so Peacekeeper Green we couldn't make the decision and were too
overwhelmed to put on a wedding."*

*Then nodding toward the group, the husband said, "Actually,
this group got together and put on the wedding for us."*

**Minuses:** Contemplative, indecisive, no sense of urgency, easily
overwhelmed, lack planning to accomplish. Commitment phobic, let's just leave things the way they are, or if it ain't broke don't
fix it.

*I don't know this couple but I know the mother of the Peacekeeper
son. She threatens to check the Guinness Book of World Records
to see if her son and his green girlfriend win the record for dating
the longest. They started dating in high school are now in their
early forties. He has been transferred twice and she has followed
him both times, each getting a separate apartment.*

Every couple is unique. Family of origin, childhood, life experience, and education are a few factors that make up the sum
total of each couple. Some combinations work better than others. Knowing each partner's type and all the new information
this section has provided should help you to have constructive
conversations about where you are and where you'd like to be in
this partnership. The next chapter offers action steps for moving
forward.

# CHAPTER 8

# ACTION PLAN FOR A WINNING COMBO

Since you are reading this book, an assumption might be made that you are the spouse trying to enrich, encourage, or—worst case scenario—save the marriage. Even if you are the only one who knows the concepts in this book, there is hope. Change starts with you anyway. You are the only adult on the planet you have control over. Can we influence others for good? Absolutely, but controlling and trying to charge another is entirely different from influencing and role modeling. Interpersonal communication and understanding, using your knowledge of the personality types well, evoke the greatest response.

## ACTION STEP BASICS

Study every description and chart in this book about you. Be intentional. Make a list of your personality traits you want to strengthen and those you want to diminish or just plain dump. Ask yourself what personality traits are enriching your marriage and what are the detractors? Be very conscientious and intentional about reducing the detractors. At this point honestly assess the condition of your marriage. Remember the story of the two triangles? Let's use those three loose groupings to assess your marriage. Is your marriage in the Enrichment Group? Or are you in the Discouraged and Frustrated Group, needing tips, tools, and techniques to manage it more lovingly? Or is your marriage in the Self-Centered/Fear Based (in-trouble) Group? Let me say right here, marriages in Group three and some in Group two need outside professional help.

Any marriage that is fear based needs professional help. Start looking for the right counseling today. But if you are in group three or two, knowing your personality type and that of your spouse will be an excellent tool to have as you work with a professional.

If you care enough about yourself and the relationship to be intentional and work the plan, you will see positive changes especially in yourself. Honest change starts with you. Take an unbiased accounting of YOU. As I advised above, make a list. What do you do that is helpful to the marriage and what is destructive? Which list is longer? If you want different results you need to do something different. Change YOU and change the environment. Commit to making your helpful list longer and the destructive list shorter. Here are some tips to accomplish this.

- Be intentional about communicating to yourself and spouse things that are enriching versus diminishing. The power of life and death is in the tongue. Speak life to your life.

- Beware of slips that discourage or diminish you or your mate. Bring it out in the open and apologize. Yes, even to yourself. If you are worried about being seen talking to yourself then pick up the phone. The art of fake works here.

- Exercise compassion. Pay attention to your thoughts and actions. Watch the negative thought patterns. Eliminate blame placing, criticism, and guilt tripping. Immediately upon realizing you've thought a negative, replace it with a positive. Give both you and your spouse the benefit of the doubt; error on the side of grace.

■ If you haven't fixed you, getting rid of your partner will not fix the problem.

There will be a positive effect on the marriage and family when you work on you in conjunction with increasing your awareness and desire to understand and meet the needs of others.

After finishing this book you will be able to understand and begin to speak the language of the four personality types. You are always going to speak from your own first and second personality types the most fluently. You will understand and identify with the people in your same type the most. But your new knowledge and skills will be a valuable tool for relating to the other personality types. Positive change will come.

## KEY ACTION STEPS FOR SUCCESS

Ask your spouse to have a brief visit weekly or biweekly, depending on your schedules, to share some insights you have gained. Tell your spouse about this book. Explain that you are excited, encouraged, hopeful, or whatever adjective best suits your spouse's personality type, and the state of your marriage in the current moment. Find some quality time. Start with ten to fifteen minutes and work toward longer visits. I use the term **visit** here because meeting is formal and businesslike; session sounds like therapy or the gym, and appointment reminds us of the dentist. Visit with your spouse. This is the most important human relationship you have. Give your time together respect and the special treatment it deserves. At least offer a beverage. It says I care and this is important to me.

### First Visit

Do not talk about your spouse first. Stick with the topic you are the world's leading expert on—YOU. Tell him or her some things you have learned about yourself as they pertain to adding value to the marriage. The condition of the marriage and your current relationship at this first visit will have to guide how much you want to be vulnerable and share regarding your future work on yourself. Remember, present what you want your spouse to know about you in a manner or format that best fits his or her personality type.

If you want him or her to hear you, then you must try to speak your mate's personality type language. A job well begun is half done. If you want to get to visit two, stay on the positive side. Stick to the topic. Resist the temptation to heal your injustices or hurts in this visit.

### Deal Breaker

This visit is not the time to unload every blind spot, weakness, or bad news trait you've read about your spouse in the whole book. This first visit is about you. It is an honest, authentic sharing of what you've learned about you that will help the marriage. Be honest and truthful about what you have learned about yourself. Hopefully, your spouse will want to know more and possibly find out his or her personality type. DO NOT GIVE THAT AWAY! Give your mate the book to find out.

### Future Visits

If your spouse has learned his or her personality type then ask him/her to look over the marriage section in the book and decide the topic for the next visit. The chart on Meeting Emotional Needs is a foundational place to start. Or the Similarity and Difference charts are always good for a candid discussion. You will know if visit two went well if there are plans for visit three and so on.

## ACTION STEPS FOR VISITS THAT ENRICH THE MARRIAGE

### Get Your Priorities Straight

It might seem at first like you are doing all the work. Stop the tapes that say, "Poor me, this is unequal, not balanced; why do I have to do everything?" or "I'm the only one who cares or I didn't cause this anyway." Truthfully if you have this book in the first place, there is probably some need somewhere. So step up, take the lead. This is for the good of the relationship, not just you. Put the marriage first. Ask yourself before every visit: How will our conversation help to enrich our marriage? Ask your mate to list what makes him/her feel loved and special. Make sure every day you say or do one of the things on the list. If you don't feel like your spouse deserves it, do it anyway. It's good for your mate, the marriage, and you. Eventually make a list for yourself. Ask if you can present your list at a future visit. Your mate's answer will give you some idea of how this whole new attempt on your part to increase understanding and communication is working. If you get a no answer, keep on keeping on; don't get discouraged. Wait a few visits and try again. If you continue to get no for an answer, you might need the help of a third-party professional.

### Listen More Than Talk

Yes, I know that just above I recommended you start the early visits by telling what you've learned from this book that will help the marriage. You did this to make it safe for your spouse. You were forthcoming but not accusatory. You simply stated what parts of your personality you planned to work on to edify the marriage. You DID NOT talk about your spouse at this time. Your goal was just to talk about you and your plan for changing yourself. Hopefully, your actions made your mate feel safe enough to want to start healthy interpersonal communication, and visits have become an important part of your married life. It is the quality of these visits that now becomes very critical.

## QUALITY VISITS

The tougher the issue your spouse is sharing, the more you need to listen. Watch for body language and make eye contact.

Engage with head nods, a very brief comment that shows you are listening, and body language from you that says "I'm present and engaged." Let your mate know you hear the feelings behind the words he or she is saying.

If your mate shares how your actions or reactions affect your mate, it is much harder to separate your mate's feelings from your own reactions. Wanting to defend yourself here will change the situation to a battle of words versus an opportunity to maybe get some issues out on the table and eventually resolve them. This time, exercise extreme will power and try to get to your mate's feelings before you start to defend yourself. This is not easy but it can be done and must be done to move on to future visits that are not just another *did so, did not, are so, are not* battle of words. Listening is the most important part of any communication and it is where we all need to grow the most. Listen until you know the feelings of your mate and then ask if you might say what you think you heard. LISTEN when you get feedback to see if you are tracking with your mate's feelings and message.

## ADDITIONAL INFORMATION

In the Coworker section in Chapter 16, there are two charts that are worth using in one or two of your visits. See Silent Questions Team Members are asking. Talk with each other about your personal silent questions as they relate to your marriage. Are you meeting each other's needs in this area?

The other chart is entitled, Types under Adverse Conditions. Study this chart and read the paragraph below it for marriages.

Have a candid discussion about where each of you goes in stressful situations. Do you stay in your strengths or go to your blind spots. If you go to your blind spots, how does that affect the marriage? Remember this is an opportunity to move forward in love, not a time to win a point for your side.

## SUMMARY

This section started with the current divorce statistic. Why start negative? No couple marries and plans to become a divorce statistic. We never plan to fail in anything; but without intentionality, caring, and general maintenance, neglect can happen fast. Misunderstanding our mate or spouse-to-be, getting discouraged and shutting down communication, or getting angry and wanting to get even are ways to move toward a failed marriage.

There is hope. If one or both of you have read this book to this point, you now have new tools to use for enhanced communication. Work your action plan. Use the charts. Start talking and listening. Pray together. People who are prayed for do better, and you obviously want to strengthen your marriage, or you would not be reading this. If only one of you prays, one is better than none. You just improved the odds. Remember what made you fall in love in the first place. Stop the negative tapes and reread all the strengths of your mate and focus on those. Do not even glance at the blind spots; you've got those down pat. The next time you are with your mate, say thank you for one of his or her strengths and tell how it enriches the marriage. Aim for more visits, and each time try to improve the quality.

If there is a setback visit, don't give up. Try again. Remember the good, bad, and maybe even the ugly visits are a process. This is a journey.

There will be many stops and starts on this road to mutual respect, cherishing, and intimacy. Power struggles, conflicts, and setbacks with all their frustration and pain are keys for growth and healing for each of you and the marriage. Many relationships can in the worst case scenario be saved or enriched by giving unconditional love and understanding.

Love was there once. It may not be dead, just buried alive. If you think professional guidance would help, get it. Whatever the cost, it's less expensive than a divorce that would tear at your heart and soul. First, give until you can't give anymore, and you might rediscover love.

*Family is a great gift indeed*
*But in its bounds there's a fact to concede.*
*Mother, father, sister, brother,*
*We must let these others*
*Have freedom apart to succeed.*

# FAMILY

## *Can't Live With Them,*
## *Can't Live Without Them*

The family, what do those two little words evoke in your mind? Does it include your parents, grandparents, aunts, uncles and cousins—your typical extended family? Or do you flash to your husband and children, your immediate family? Maybe it's parents and siblings if you have no family of your own yet. Or possibly just your children come to mind. Whatever the family means to you, it is usually multiple people and lots of different personalities with whom to deal. Admittedly, we all do better with some more than others.

In this section you will learn about parents, siblings, and other adult relatives. A second part of The Family section will have a strong emphasis on the children in your life. To understand your adult family members, think about what you have just learned in the YOU section. What are, or were (if deceased), your parents' personality types? How about siblings? If you don't know, take the Assessment again and answer the way you think they would answer. Maybe you won't be completely right, but I'll bet you'll be close and possibly have a couple of "aha" moments.

The adults in your family whose personality types are the most different from yours are probably the ones you understand the least and trouble you the most. More than once I've heard, "You can pick your friends and divorce a spouse but you are stuck with your family." There is truth here, so let's get to know and understand this adult family. Let's learn to live with them because there is truth in saying we really can't live without them. Family is at our foundational core.

One of my certified People Skills trainers specializes in family reunions. She is a trainer for a major network marketing company, and people in her audiences kept saying, "You've just got to tell my whole family what you just told us. It will help a ton and sure explains a lot." So, one family at a time, she is creating understanding, increasing harmony, and improving family dynamics through understanding personality types.

A word is necessary here about functional and dysfunctional families. Please do not let present-day television families help you define normal families. Ozzie and Harriet are sadly gone, their show replaced by shows that give even fewer clues to what a "normal" family looks like. Many characters are portrayed as operating in the weakness areas or blind spots of their personalities versus their strengths.

Understanding personality types is extremely beneficial in families. However, if substance abuse, physical or verbal abuse, neglect, constant fear, abandonment, or other dysfunctions are or were present, there are greater issues with which to deal. These family issues, old or current, require professional help. When dealing with these issues, remember your core personality type and be true to who you are. When dealing with a dysfunctional family member it will help you to know the person's core personality, but current dysfunction can overshadow personality type.

# CHAPTER 9

# WHERE ARE THEY COMING FROM?

As you can see in the table on the next page, a greater portion of the population is either a Planner or a Peacekeeper. Maybe that will help you determine your relatives' personality types. Ask yourself whether they are relationship oriented or would they rather just exclude people and get the job done. Knowing how they feel about change and their communication style of asking versus telling will help you zero in on a type. Read the "Check This Out" section of this chapter for more ways to determine your adult relatives' types.

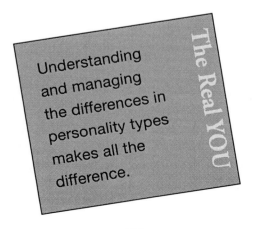

Understanding and managing the differences in personality types makes all the difference.

The Real YOU

# UNDERSTANDING THE ADULTS IN YOUR FAMILY

## MUST KNOW

| Yellow Promoter | Blue Planner |
|---|---|
| 19% of total population | 35% of total population |
| Female 65%—male 35% | Male 60%—female 40% |
| Heart makes decision—emotion based | Brain makes decision—logic based |
| Direct communicator— tells vs. asks | Indirect communicator— asks vs. tells |
| Prefers relationships over tasks | Prefers tasks over relating with others |
| More extroverts than introverts | Close split/extroverts and introverts |
| Seeks change | Avoids change |
| **Red Producer** | **Green Peacekeeper** |
| 14% of total population | 32% of total population |
| Male 60%—female 40% | Female 65%—male 35% |
| Brain makes decision—logic based | Heart makes decision—emotion based |
| Direct communicator— tells vs. asks | Indirect communicator— asks vs. tells |
| Prefers tasks over relating with others | Prefers relationships over tasks |
| More extroverts than introverts | Close split/extroverts and introverts |
| Seeks change | Avoids change |

## CHECK THIS OUT

If you are a Promoter or a Peacekeeper, you are not likely to mind the course I'm about to take you on. Planners, you probably won't like this, but it will be good for you. Planners always need to work on being more flexible. This is your chance. Producers usually think they know how it should be done and I'm sure my Promoter actions here are not what you would do. But Producers, here's the deal . . . the end justifies the means, and I know you can handle that.

There are a series of pages or charts I want you to look at throughout the book to help you understand the person or persons in your family who may be moderately annoying you as well as those at the end of the spectrum who are driving you crazy. If you don't have any such persons, realize you are in the minority. Thank God and skip ahead.

Re-read the YOU section of the book that describes the personality type of the relative you want to understand better. Are you two totally opposite? If so, of course you never "got" the person and have totally different life approaches.

Go to the Marriage section to review the series of charts called, Similarities and Differences. Once you've figured out the personality type of your challenging adult relative, go find the chart with your personality type that matches up with that person's. This should begin to give you some insight.

While you are in the Marriage section, read these two charts: Meeting your Mate's Needs (Switch out mate for your relative's name.) and Insights into My Mate's Personality Type.

The next stop on this book treasure hunt is the Coworker section. Here you will find three helpful charts: Customize Connections, Silent Questions, and Types under Adverse Conditions. By now you should be seeing this relative in a new light—an illumination that gives you ideas and a new resolve on how to deal with this person. For any relationship to be successful, you need understanding; and when you add in attempting to communicate with them in their personality type languages, you've got a great start. This relationship may not give you instant gratification but you are a better person for trying to understand and improve the relationship. As you read the next section about the children, keep the adult relatives in mind. Remember, adults are just grown-up kids. Read, enjoy, and revert to your youth.

# CHAPTER 10

# HELP! I DON'T UNDERSTAND THIS CHILD

## HAVE YOU EVER THOUGHT:

- This child is not at all like me.
- Where did this kid come from?
- How can kids raised in the same family be so different?
- I'm not like that at all.
- I'd never do it that way.
- I don't understand this child!

This section responds to these thoughts and questions. Since there is no one exactly like you, no one of the exact hue as you, why is it so difficult to accept that none of the children in your life are just like you? It is not our similarities that cause most of the frustration when working with children; it is the differences. Learning about the personalities of the children in your life and knowing your core personality helps you to understand and improve the quality of those relationships.

I am writing this chapter as a spokesperson for children. The purpose is to aid adults in raising children in the way God intended them to be. When we train them with an understanding of who they are, we will help develop them into the adults they can be. Most adults want to understand and meet the personality needs of children. They just don't understand or speak the language of personality types. After reading this book a person will be able to understand and speak the language of the four personality types.

We are always going to speak most fluently in our own personality language. We understand and identify with the people with our same personality type the most. But let's learn three other new personality languages.

Even if you struggle, try speaking the language of the personality type of the child with whom you are working. I have a file full of correspondence from adults who shared success stories about finally understanding the child with whom they were struggling. When you speak the language of someone's personality type, that individual hears the language of understanding and love.

As I speak to audiences of parents and teachers, they find it easy to identify the Promoter and Producer children. The Planners and the Peacekeepers often take a bit more analyzing. The child you are trying to understand may wear not one but two T-shirts rather consistently. This factor is to be considered.

If you have very young children, you may not be able to identify their personality types just yet. However, many of my friends are grandmothers, and most of them know their grandchildren's personality types around the first year. Gramma Standley said, "Our newest grandbaby is definitely a Producer. He gives us a look that says, 'Enjoy being in charge while you can, soon I'm taking over.'"

Another grandmother, Nana Nelson, reported, "Joshua is for sure a Planner, his Tonka trucks are always in a perfectly straight line across the room, and he does not like them to be out of order. I have ten grandchildren, and this one at three is the most orderly and serious of them all."

My friend Sharon described her week of babysitting for her three grandchildren like this: "Well, Alex was her usual in-charge Producer self. I'm sure that girl is going to be president some day. T.J. entertained me all week with his wild stories and sparkling Promoter personality. I know baby Cameron is a Peacekeeper. I've never seen a more docile contented baby in my life."

This letter came from a seminar participant, Planner Kimberly, a fourth-grade teacher:

> After your seminar I took the picture of the four personality type T-shirts to school. I taped it to my desk. Some of my students I immediately identified and wrote their names by the appropriate shirt. Over the weekend I studied your handouts and was able to identify almost all of my class. I wrote their names by the shirt they wore the most. There were still four children about whom I was confused. In the week that followed your seminar I paid special attention to my unidentified four. Two I finally figured out were Planners, but since both of them had rather disorganized desks much of the time, they stumped me for a while. When I questioned Carrie about the messy desk I knew she was a Planner. She said, "I want a clean desk. I want it perfect. I hate things messy. I have a big desk at home, and I keep it just right. But this one is too small, and there are too many books and things to fit right so I just gave up."
>
> My last two unidentified students were born drug babies and come from horrendous backgrounds. Each has severe emotional problems. I remember you said that children like this were often difficult, if not impossible, to identify. These two need all the love and understanding they can get. I'll keep working on it.

Thank you on behalf of the children. Your seminar really helped me to do a better job with each individual personality in my class. I know this is a Planner thing, but I've even listed what I think are shades of their group colors.

As you read the next section with specific children in mind, remember to rule out personalities that don't fit the child. You can keep a list of certain personality characteristics that fit the child you are trying to identify. You will soon know the personality type or the T-shirt the child you are thinking about wears most of the time.

CHAPTER 11

# WHICH T-SHIRT IS YOUR CHILD WEARING?

 **PERKY PROMOTERS/YELLOW/SPRINGS**

My friend Linda, a pediatric nurse in a hospital, said she can usually spot this personality group even in the newborn section. She claimed there is a perky attitude and energy for the joy of life in these newborns. Laughingly she said, "It's like they are looking at me and saying, 'Hey, this life stuff is great! Aren't you glad I'm here?' Perky Promoters like life and themselves unless someone convinces them of the contrary.

Linda summed up Perky Promoter children well. They have a zest for life that spills energy and joy to those around them. They have a beckoning call to join them. Life is for living—let the fun begin.

My girlfriend Diane described her eighteen-month-old Promoter grandson this way. When Collin's mom is away and she calls to talk to him, because he has no verbal language to communicate with her, upon hearing her voice, he puts the phone down and wiggles his whole body with joy.

My friend Phil describes his yellow son, Cole, who is six, in this way: "Cole brings joy to the end of my workday. He stands in the driveway, and the minute he sees my car, he does the dance of football players in the end zone and yells, 'Daddy's home, yeah!' Cole has a gusto about him that says: Life is to be lived to the fullest. Let's not miss anything."

The Perky Promoters are busy, animated, fast-paced children. Their activities are often random and scattered. These children are easily distracted because life is so wondrous, and they do not want to miss a thing. For this yellow Promoter group, life is to be experienced in an all-out, go-for-the-gusto blitz. They want to take everyone they encounter along for the ride. These are free-spirited children. They have huge imaginations and the courage to risk and go for it. This group isn't always sure where they are going, but they are going. They represent the saying, "I don't know where I'm going but I'm making great time!"

These are highly verbal children. They like words and are usually very articulate even as small children. Their gifts of having big hearts and loving people help them express their emotions and feelings. And these children have strong emotions and feel deeply! They have a sixth sense about people around them.

These children express what they are feeling and what others might be feeling. Promoters are often very candid and tell it like it is. They don't always act on what they feel, but they will express it. Often these children are better talkers than doers.

An idea a minute pops into the heads of these children. They are great at brainstorming and thinking up wild and crazy schemes. Some are better at implementing than others. Starting is fun. They can rise to the challenge and thrill. They start something, figure out: "Hey, I can do this," and stop. They stop because now they've "been there and done that." They have met the challenge, and that's enough for them. Ideas are their specialty, starts are next, and finishes are last for most of this group. Mastery is unimportant. Often completion seems boring and repetitious, and these children do not do anything boring if they can help it.

Following through can be difficult for these children. Several factors come into play here:

- Having high energy.

- Not liking routine or repetition.

- Having too many ideas to focus on one.

- Being so busy experiencing and promoting life, they can't stay in one place too long.

- They bore easily and can be impulsive.

- Running the race of life is a sprint not a marathon for Perky Promoters.

In one of my seminars recently, a mother rushed up afterwards and said, "Last week I had my child tested to see if she had attention deficit disorder or was hyperactive. The test said she was neither. I still wondered what was wrong with her. She is so active, unfocused, and all over the place. Now I know there is absolutely nothing wrong with her. She is a very bright-yellow Promoter."

**Adults Need to Understand This about Perky Promoters:**

- We like life to be fun.

- For emotional growth we need lots of A's.

  ☞ Attention—Watch me, listen to me.

  ☞ Approval—Did I do "good"? I need to know.

  ☞ Affection—I'm a kid who operates with my heart. Hug me, love me.

  ☞ Audience—Please watch me play out my life

  ☞ Applause—I'm a performer. I need to see and hear your approval.

  ☞ Acceptance—Don't leave me out! I must be included.

☞ Affirmations—Keep telling me how wonderful I am. I live for praise.

- Our specialties
    - ☞ Having a good time
    - ☞ Helping others to have a good time
    - ☞ Encouraging others to reach full potential
    - ☞ Talking to anyone about anything
    - ☞ Bubbling personality
    - ☞ Entertaining people
    - ☞ Funny
    - ☞ Fun friend
    - ☞ Giving compelling reason to get what we want
    - ☞ Considering others' feelings
- What makes us sad
    - ☞ Being left out
    - ☞ Thinking no one likes us
    - ☞ People who say mean things about us
    - ☞ Mean people
    - ☞ Being yelled at for not having our "act together"
    - ☞ Losing things, and we do it a lot!
- Fears
    - ☞ Not being popular
    - ☞ Strict rules
    - ☞ Being bored

☞ No freedom

☞ No fun

☞ No friends

☞ Mean people

☞

- What is fun for us
  ☞ Doing things with friends

  ☞ Talking to friends at school or on the phone

  ☞ Just being with our friends

  ☞ Vacation with our family and other families with kids

  ☞ Special trips with friends

  ☞ Birthday parties, especially our own

  ☞ Getting to do special things like performing in plays and shows

  ☞ Being on teams that go for pizza after the game

- Help us with
  ☞ Organizing time and materials

  ☞ Being too optimistic

  ☞ Being too gullible

  ☞ Being too accepting

  ☞ Emotionally flying all over the place

  ☞ Telling the truth

  ☞ Planning ahead

## ATTENTION GROWN-UPS: THIS IS IMPORTANT STUFF!

## WANTS AND NEEDS

### Attention

These children need more attention than most parents realize. They never can hear enough words of encouragement or praise. This group is like puppies, jumping around your ankles waiting for you to pat them on the head and say "atta girl" or "atta boy," just because they exist. Promoters need lots of pats on the head for encouragement and hugs to keep them going. Affirmations that say they are good and that you love them—not for what they do, but because they exist—are music to their ears.

Because this group is not as task oriented as they are relationship oriented, as parents you may have to focus your praise on their character qualities versus their performances and results. Mention their character qualities such as friendliness, generosity, including others, humor, optimism, and how much fun you have with them. Please don't hold back your words of affirmation until your child performs a home task or a school task well. This child thrives on praise. Verbal affirmations are vital to meeting the attention needs for this child.

All children say, "Watch me, Mommy. Watch me, Daddy." But this group needs an audience as they unfold their life drama. Most of these children like spotlight time where they can be the center of attention. Many of these children have a great sense of humor. Some are comedians. Parents describe these kids as hams, cut-ups, thespians, or clowns. You can often find the class clown among this group. They entertain everyone and definitely get an A in social life.

As an elementary school teacher I found the yellow Promoter group generally liked "Show and Tell." They always had something to say. I call this story "A Star Is Born."

Charlynn was a charming, bright-yellow Promoter. She was in my kindergarten class. At six years of age, life was a play, and she held the starring role. For Charlynn the "Show and Tell" time was her forum. I knew I could always count on Charlynn to have something to say. She was naturally articulate and, at a tender age, knew how to hold the attention of an audience. Promoters are naturally good storytellers. Charlynn had a very big imagination. She made her family and her dog Muffin larger than life.

To hear Charlynn share her glamorous family life, you would think it was a movie script. In fact, she had just a normal, average family with a below-average dog. She used her charming wit to transform the ordinary into the extraordinary.

One of my challenges as her teacher was to help her separate fact from fiction. Promoting children can inflate and exaggerate stories to make them more exciting and make themselves look more important than they are. Image is important to some Promoter children. Sometimes they will even resort to lying to make things bigger and more important than they are. This personality group has a strong awareness of social standing and status.

Usually Promoters are easy to spot. They are not only highly verbal and vocal, they are also visual. They will be seen animatedly moving with sweeping gestures and often wearing the latest style with flash and pizzazz. This group has flair and panache. Most are not shy about standing out in a crowd. Often that is precisely their motive. They like to be in style. Cutting-edge fashions and brand-name clothing are important to most of these children and teenagers.

## Popularity

These yellow Promoter children are people magnets. They have a "come one, come all" attitude and "more is always merrier." They are Pied Pipers because the music of their lives is lively, upbeat, and invites others to join in the merriment. Engaging and entertaining, they are great at influencing others to join in their work or play. Think about Tom Sawyer and Huck Finn. Who watched and munched on an apple while his friend took over the painting?

Our friends, Planner Don and Peacekeeper Ann laughingly describe being the parents of a Promoter. "From a very early age Josh had a lot happening. Because of him our house was a hive of activity. The phone rang more for him than for anyone else. Most of the knocking at the door was for Josh. He always had twice as many friends around as our other kids." Josh was a busy boy with an active social life to maintain.

Our son Tyler is also a perky Promoter. As a young child people called him "Tyler the Smiler." Plus he is a charmer. He had developed social skills very young and was always at ease with adult as well as peers. He charmed his way into everyone's heart. There was always an upbeat energy when Tyler was around.

When Tyler was in elementary school I used to wait until he got home to run the boring errands. When he was with me it turned boring into fun adventure. He pointed out things I had never seen before. He helped me laugh at myself on those "whatever can go wrong will go wrong" days. It seemed I was always the one who got the shopping cart with the loud crazy wheel or the leaky carton of milk. If anyone was going to drop a carton of eggs on brand new shoes, it was me.

We were so much alike it was a great time for me to show him the good news and the bad news about being who we were. However, as he got older, one-on-one time with Tyler was rare. His friends were always around or calling. As a teenager it seemed to our family that his friends were his life.

Relationships, especially with peers, are often more important than anything else to these children. Friendships and popularity are high on the list for Promoters. School for this group is first about interacting with their friends often, with the academics coming in second. Parents of Perky Promoters state that perky isn't 100 percent. These upbeat children can roller coaster from on top of the world to the bottom in record time. Often the trigger point is criticism, exclusion, or a perceived slight by a friend. Fortunately, like the roller coaster, their downs might be deep but usually not long.

Carrie is a darling, teenage yellow Promoter. She has so many boyfriends, I can't keep up. I asked her mother if Carrie is always the heartbreaker. Her mom said it's about fifty/fifty. The cycle is: one minute this is "Mr. Right," and the next minute her heart is broken, followed by dramatic tears and, of course, a new boyfriend. Life is again a joyous happening. Her dad says her theme song is, "If You Can't Be with the One You Love, Love the One You're With."

## Flexibility

A spring is flexible, and Promoter children and teenagers want flexibility in their lives. From meals to rules to school, this group wants versatility. This group likes to reinvent the wheel. They often do something a different way each time. Tight boundaries and rigid rules are very difficult for this group to follow. The teen years can be difficult for parents and these children. After all, this yellow Promoter group believes rules are made to be broken. Because life is meant to be fun and peer relationships are at the top of their priority list, then it follows that schoolwork and chores at home barely make the list—and certainly not as priorities. Some of these children are just plain wild. They are going to experience life and all it brings. Hedonistic, narcissistic, and out-of-control behavior can happen to some of these kids. The family takes the brunt of their ugly behavior while they use their charm on everyone else. Once the difficult years are over, these Promoters will again bring their joy and energy back to the family. Relationships are paramount to Promoters. They need family and friends.

# GOOD NEWS/BAD NEWS

| Good News | Bad News |
|---|---|
| Charming | Can be phony and cunning |
| Entertaining story tellers | Beware of minnows that suddenly grow into whales as the story progresses |
| Flexible | Too loose to contain—mercurial |
| Positive and optimistic | Unrealistic dreamer |
| Friendly | Self-serving, using popularity to get what they want |
| Enthusiastic volunteer | Uncommitted, unreliable—drops the ball |
| Creative ideas | No focus or follow through |
| Delightful | More fluff than substance |
| Fun-loving | Shallow and foolish |
| Spontaneous | Impulsive and forgetful |
| Unique | Nonconforming |
| Excellent communication skills | Nonstop talking |

# PROMOTERS

| Teenage Promoters | |
|---|---|
| Fun | Friends are more important that family |
| Cheerleaders of life | Wild child |
| Joyful | Rebellious toward rules and boundaries |
| Energetic | Total flake |
| Charming | Superficial and tells you what you want to hear |
| Encourager | Rebellious in appearance |
| Magnetism | Vain and disingenuous |
| Hangout house | Enlist the whole family in their life |
| Social whirl | Grabbing all the attention and hogging the spotlight |
| Fast paced | Exhausting for others to be around |

##  PRECISE PLANNERS/BLUE/BOX

As a teacher, I found most Planner children a blessing to have in my classroom. These are dependable, dutiful, responsible children. Even the ones who struggled academically were good kids, diligently taking it one step at a time, trying to get it right.

On the whole, this precise group does not have discipline problems. Rebellion in school would go against their conforming, rule-following nature. Are Planners perfect angels all the time in school? No, but the format of school is usually a comfort zone for these children and an arena that meets many of their needs, so they fit.

They like the routine of the daily schedule. Things are put in writing, and they know what's expected of them. These children like a life that is systematic and orderly, and school is generally one of those places. The consistency of the school day appeals to these boundary-desiring children.

Planners don't like to be late. Tardiness for this group represents breaking rules, irresponsibility, and disorganization. These are all traits that go against the grain of these "by the book" children.

Planner children as a group manage time and materials very well. The neatest desk awards usually go to students in this group. They don't like clutter, chaos, or things out of place. This group coined the phrase "a place for everything and everything in its place." And most of them stick to it. At the end of the year, these students still had all twenty-four crayons in the twenty-four pack, and few were broken. As compared to most of Promoter students who were down to several broken stubs of the less desirable colors.

Precise Planners can take their strong desire to get it right to the next level—perfectionism. Being analytical and detail oriented, these kids know what "right" should look like. The logical voice in their heads says, "Getting life right all the time is not possible." But many in this group still have to give it their best shot.

There are seemingly opposing goals in both the adult and child version of the Planner. On one side there is a strong desire for perfection, but on the other their logic-based minds say, "It can't happen." Perfection and pessimism seem to surround Planners. Frustration, discouragement, and negativity are common feelings for these children. They want to get it perfect, but history, their own data, and logic say it won't happen. So enters "gloom and doom time." Tapes in their heads say, "I'll never get it right. I'm a huge failure." These are the "black clouds overhead" times that Planners experience.

Tears of frustration poured over six-year-old Randy's chubby cheeks. He had spent the whole morning learning to tie his shoes. He had finally mastered the bow but the laces wouldn't stay tied. Standing in the kitchen with not one but two untied shoes, he declared that, "life was just not fair," and stormed into his bedroom.

I asked his mother how she was going to handle it, and she said, "I'm not. He'll stay in his room having a pity party and then he will finish that and start trying again to tie the perfect bow. This child is tightly and intensely made. His day is a roller coaster of emotions. He is caught between his perfectionism and his pessimism. He sets his standards so high that when he fails it's the end of the world. Poor Randy, I hope he finds middle ground soon."

Tightly and intensely made is a good description for many in this group. From the homework papers that aren't neat enough, to projects that don't turn out perfectly, these children set high standards for themselves. They put pressure on themselves and become upset and discouraged when things don't turn out the way they had planned.

Planners work and play intensely. Toys or activities with many parts and details appeal to Planners. They have the ability to focus and really stick with a project, becoming absorbed in and oblivious to the world around them. Liking the process and enjoying developing systems, they enjoy playing with toys with lots of pieces—Legos, puzzles, Tinkertoys, and Erector Sets. Girls like the whole Dream House, with the kitchen complete with every dish, appliance, and pan. Barbie's accessories are usually more enjoyable for this blue Planner than Barbie.

## Adults Need to Understand This about Precise Planners:

- We like a life where things are right, with as few mistakes and goofs as possible.
- For emotional growth we need . . .
  - ☞ appreciation for the way we think it through and try to get it right.
  - ☞ appreciation for quality work.
  - ☞ appreciation for being responsible.
  - ☞ to belong.
  - ☞ acceptance in groups.
  - ☞ stability.
  - ☞ security.
  - ☞ a strategy the includes key success factors.
- Our specialties are . . .
  - ☞ organization.
  - ☞ solving problems with practical solutions.
  - ☞ high standards and ideals.
  - ☞ thoughtfulness.
  - ☞ dependability.
  - ☞ honesty.
  - ☞ following rules.
  - ☞ independent thinking.

- What makes us sad or mad is . . .

  ☞ craziness in life.

  ☞ when people don't do it right, like cheating and sloppiness.

  ☞ when no one seems to care about correcting things.

  ☞ when people are flakes, goof-offs, or lazy.

  ☞ disorganization.

- We fear . . .

  ☞ making mistakes.

  ☞ not being understood.

  ☞ not being accepted.

  ☞ having to do something poorly or only halfway.

  ☞ having other people play with or touch our things and mess them up.

- We enjoy . . .

  ☞ vacations with our families.

  ☞ friends doing something together.

  ☞ going to clubs and groups where it's organized and with opportunities for projects and earning awards.

  ☞ working on a project in a place where we have space.

  ☞ school sometimes.

  ☞ some sports teams but not with a lot of kids that just want to mess around.

- Help us with . . .

  ☞ overcoming negativity.

  ☞ finding the positive things is life.

☞ flexibility.

☞ seeing what is right about a situation versus what's wrong.

☞ increasing our tolerance of others.

☞ being less rigid.

## ATTENTION GROWN-UPS: THIS IS IMPORTANT STUFF!

## WANTS AND NEEDS
### Order, Planning, and Routine

My friend Anne is a single mom. She and her son (twelve) and daughter (ten) are all Precise Planners. Visiting their home anytime, day or night, is amazing. The house looks magazine perfect, and no matter what activity they are engaged in, there is no mess. At Halloween they carve pumpkins and make candy apples without seeds and sticky on the floor. They dye Easter eggs without colored stains anywhere, and even Christmas morning the living room doesn't look like a hurricane ripped through.

Anne says her hardest job as a parent to these Planner kids is not to make them do things right, but to encourage them to lighten up and let their standards have some flexibility. She states, "My children put way more pressure on themselves to get it right than I ever would put on them. I'm an uptight Planner, too, but I've had to loosen up because my two kids are both such perfectionists. Someone around here has to lighten up and go with the flow."

Going with the flow is often hard for Planners because flowing is just too spontaneous and risky. Most Planners don't like change and aren't too excited about a lot of risky situations. "Make a plan, and work the plan," fits most blue group lifestyles. Planners claim they can be spontaneous if you give them enough time!

## Being Part of the System

Planners need for order comes into play in their need to be part of systems. Organizations with structure, rules, charts, or guidelines that tell Planners exactly what to do and how to do it appeal to this group. Blue Planner children actually like directions on a box, and they read them. In an attempt to get it right, this group believes that directions might help. A systematic organization like Scouting or Camp Fire Girls attracts Planners.

Belonging to an organization, a family, a school, a church or synagogue, and a community meets the needs for affiliation in these children. They like being members of things. Planner children are the backbones of organizations. They are the ones who attend regularly and do the work it takes to move to the next level. They are often the group leader's dream participants. They follow the rules, do their part, and then some. Planners are servants at heart—hard workers who would not dream of letting others carry their share of the load. You can count on Planners to do their part and do it well.

The three boys I know who have attained the honor of Eagle Scout are all blue Planners. The last two bar mitzvahs and one bas mitzvah I know about were all from the blue Planner group. These accomplishments take determination, dependability, and stick-to-itiveness, and this group has it. They thrive on being part of an organized system.

## To Be Appreciated

Remember you are dealing with perfectionists, precise Planners. They don't like to generalize about or round off anything.

Affirm them, praise them, and let them know how much you appreciate them in an exact and precise manner. Planners love things in writing. When putting it in writing, be specific. Give details, focus on quality, and describe the when, where, why, and how of exactly what you appreciate about your Planner child.

This group likes the past. History is very important to them, and so is personal history. Create it for them with keepsakes, photo albums, cards, and notes that will become part of their history.

My sister is a Planner. As children we shared a room. She saved stuff—the napkin from her first Brownie tea, report cards, and awards. Every note, Valentine, and corsage she ever received was neatly and carefully filed, pasted, or pressed into the living memories of her life. Her side of the room reflected who she was. Bookcases, window ledges, and her bedside table created her history and portrayed a deep, caring, and organized young woman.

My side was a chaotic disaster. Being a fast-moving yellow, I winged it as I went along. What I didn't lose, I destroyed or tossed. I had no time or organizational skills to mess with stuff. My saving methods consisted of shoving it under my bed. Your Planner child is deep. They are trying to get life "right." Let them know that you know this about them, and you love and appreciate who they are.

## GOOD NEWS/BAD NEWS

| Good News | Bad News |
| --- | --- |
| Dependable and thorough | Can be slow |
| Can read a manual and figure things out to fix things | Must assemble the perfect equipment to do the job first. This can take days! |
| Sets goals | Makes too many and sets standards too high |
| Punctual | Stressed when others are late |
| Deliberate | Not spontaneous |
| Dutiful | Sensitive if not appreciated |
| Sincere | Too sensitive/hurt by insincerity |
| Problem solvers | Indecisive—analysis paralysis |
| Practical | Doesn't like a lot of new ideas |
| Deep | Moody |
| Makes few mistakes | Critical of others' mistakes |
| Realistic | Pessimistic |
| Perfectionist | Perfectionist |

## PLANNERS

| Teenage Planners | |
|---|---|
| Organized | Inflexible |
| Trustworthy | Secretive |
| Serious Student | Puts way too much pressure on self/all work, no play |
| Determined | Disappointed in their own performance |
| Steady | Self-critical |
| Observer | Withdrawn |
| Thoughtful | Hurt by insincere people |
| Sensible | Nerdy |
| Responsible | Old fashioned |
| Quality person | Goodie-goodie |
| Traditional | Hangs onto clothes even when they are old and worn |

##  POWERFUL PRODUCERS/RED/ CHECKMARK

It might have been the pain or maybe the drugs when our Powerful Producer son Matt was born, but this is what seemed to happen. His birth had been painful. Maybe it was because he was born in a three-piece suit, carrying a briefcase. He seemed to immediately take charge of the delivery room, demanding to see the credentials of all the medical staff. Somewhat satisfied with their abilities to get the results he wanted, he turned to us, the parents, looking at us with skeptical eyes that said, "Huh! I knew it. I got born to a couple of incompetents. But no problem, I'm in control here, I can shape them up in no time." He's been trying for his whole life.

Raising Powerful Producers is the best of times and the worst of times. The Bible says, "Unto whom much is given much is required." These children have incredibly strong strengths and equally strong blind spots. Generally, this red Producer group puts pressure on themselves first and then everyone else. They are driven, and they are taking themselves and everyone in their lives along for the ride. The ride isn't usually a joyride. No aimless running around the countryside for this group. Producers try not to aimlessly go anywhere, and they rarely spin their wheels.

They set goals and go for the win. These children are like racecars, driving in the fast lanes of the freeways of life and pressing for the finish line.

Producers are purposeful children. Accomplishments, achievements, and results are important to them. They are also very competitive. In early elementary school, recess games, spelling bees, and test grades give them a chance to compete and win. Later it is sporting teams, debate team, or the grade chase that challenges them to compete with winning in mind. Producer Vince Lombardi summed it up for this red group. "It isn't how you play the game, it's whether you win or lose." Planners, on the other hand, like to win but it is the process that is more important to them.

Are Producers self-confident or arrogant? Most are self-confident. Some take this wonderful attribute too far, and it becomes a limitation. Producers' traits are so strong we often don't know when they slipped over the edge to limitations. These strong personality traits can make it difficult for others to become close to Producers. They know who they are, and they know where they are going. For some of the less-driven personality types, Producers look cold, calculating, and even arrogant. Often they are not. They are just being Powerful Producers. However, the stark contrast between this personality type and the other types makes some feel inadequate and insecure.

Producers can also be perceived as bossy, aggressive, intolerant, and controlling. In their quest to produce results, they can manifest these behaviors. They can be hard on people, but they are more often hard on themselves. They can be their own worst critics. They overcome obstacles in order to complete their goals while pushing themselves to do more and more. While the Planners can never get it right, the Producers can never achieve enough.

Powerful Producers are not tolerant of incompetence in anyone. They decide how it should be and move forward. There is a bumper sticker that this red group must have started. It reads, "Be Alert, We Need More Lerts." They are alert, effective, and efficient, and they would appreciate it if everyone would be also. These kids enjoy having multiple tasks and interests. They sign up for everything from teams to chairmanships of the committees. Remember, they are driven to lead and achieve. Being busy is very important to this group. The term overachiever is custom-made for this group. For this talented, driven group it may not look like overachieving, but to the rest of the personality types their commitment level seems over the top.

In our son Matt's senior year in high school, I was certain he was going to crash and burn. He left for water polo practice at 6:00 a.m., working out with weights afterwards. Then he went on to school, where he was getting top grades. After school he had some meeting or other because he was always involved with a project to make a difference in something. If his group of friends were having any kind of a social event, from proms to ski trips, he would be organizing that also. And, of course, there was the part-time job, the girlfriend, and a few family functions. Most of the time he handled this life platter heaped with commitments with skill and confidence.

**Adults Need to Understand This about Powerful Producers:**

- We like to be in charge of our lives. We want to do it our way and get things done.

- For emotional growth we need . . .

  ☞ respect for the results we have achieved.

  ☞ credit for our talents and abilities.

  ☞ to do it ourselves.

  ☞ to be right.

  ☞ approval for the accomplishments.

☞ trust that we can do it because we have done other things well.

■ We specialize in . . .

☞ leadership.

☞ taking charge quickly in an emergency.

☞ making quick decisions.

☞ planning ahead.

☞ making things happen.

☞ getting results.

☞ trusting ourselves more than others.

☞ ingenuity.

■ It makes us mad when . . .

☞ people who do it wrong or slowly.

☞ doing something for someone who does it wrong.

☞ teachers who don't know what they are doing.

☞ people are lazy.

☞ things are out of control and people won't let us take control.

☞ coaches aren't good at coaching.

■ We fear . . .

☞ not doing well in school.

☞ not winning games and competitions at school.

☞ looking dumb or stupid.

☞ not being right.

☞ nobody cooperating with us.

☞ being bossed around.

- We enjoy . . .

    ☞ winning.

    ☞ being in charge.

    ☞ going to a special place with friends.

    ☞ big family events where we go out of town.

    ☞ having an important project and getting it done.

    ☞ competition.

- Help us with . . .

    ☞ learning to be compassionate.

    ☞ treating others with TLC.

    ☞ valuing people for who they are—not what they can do for us.

    ☞ being nonjudgmental.

    ☞ not needing to always be in control.

    ☞ not needing to always be right.

    ☞ skepticism.

    ☞ sarcasm.

## ATTENTION GROWN-UPS: THIS IS IMPORTANT STUFF!

## WANTS AND NEEDS

### To Be Right

Parent Warning: Don't tell these children it can't be done if you don't want to wave a red flag in front of them. Most Producers will take on the challenge just to prove you wrong. They like to be right!

We called our son Matt, Walking Webster, when he was young. He had an opinion on everything, and no one could convince him to the contrary once he decided what was right. Even when he was completely wrong, he almost won over people because he spoke with such confidence and authority.

Dr. James Dobson authored a book titled *The Strong-Willed Child: Birth Through Adolescence* (1995). If you are the parent of a Powerful Producer, go immediately to your nearest bookstore and get the book. Then read it! The children in the red Producer group can be opinionated and controlling. They want to do everything their way. They want to "do it themselves."

From dressing themselves to pouring their own milk, these children are independent and determined to do it their way, which of course is the right way—the only way—their way.

## Control

Dana, mother of Daniel, a strong Producer said to me one day in the park, "Watch Daniel." When all the other children his age were perfecting patty-cake and waving bye-bye, Daniel was working on snapping his fingers, pointing at a person, and then motioning him to come to him! Powerful Producers often show their leadership traits early.

Being born leaders, these children know when to take charge. They often don't know how. Instead of diplomacy and collaboration, Producers are often bossy and controlling. My husband and I presently have a red five-year-old in our life. I love to get to school early for pick-up and watch and listen to him on the playground. He is definitely the leader of the pack. He's quite bossy. I notice some of the other kids seem to accept it and take it in stride while others complain to the teacher. One day when I picked him up, the teacher said he'd been controlling all day. With a chuckle she said, "About 11:00 a.m. I thought he might stage a mutiny and take over the class."

If some Producers see a chink in your armor, they may charge. You have to be strong and get in the face of Producers sometimes. The saying, "Because I'm the mom, that's why," comes in handy with these children. They understand authority and want to have it in their lives even though they are often challenging you at each step for control.

## Opportunities to Move Ahead of the Crowd

These are not children you can expect to march in the middle. They don't have a middle mentality. Give then opportunities to succeed. Most of them are up for the challenge, if it is something that interests them. However, if they are not interested, the saying, "you can drag a horse to water but you can't make him drink," applies to parents trying to push or drag these children to do things that don't interest them. Let them pick their interests as long as they are appropriate, then stand back and enjoy the success. Powerful Producers aren't usually too good at stopping to smell the roses. Plant them, grow them, and sell them, but the simple pleasure of enjoying them isn't always easy for Producers.

Producers are generally self-confident. They are sure of what they can achieve. They are not always as sure of who they are as they are sure of what they can do. Because doing is so important, they don't stop along the way and learn what being is all about. For this red Producer group, being a great "human doing" is easy. Sometimes they have to work on developing relationships, people skills, and compassion to improve their human being part.

Recently, one of the students in my University of California, Irvine class, Producer John, said, "You're right about this people skill thing. Mine are barely decent." Then he laughed and said, "I know I need to work on mine, but I'm too busy accomplishing."

You may need to help your children develop good self-esteem. As self-confident as Producers are, they don't always enjoy good self-esteem. Self-esteem is about loving yourself because you breathe. To Producers breathing isn't much of an accomplishment. It seems everyone is doing that. They need to *do* things that set themselves apart. Help your Powerful Producer child learn the importance of being a good person and loving himself or herself for that goodness.

Taylor is the seven-year-old Powerful Producer granddaughter of my friend Kaye. One of her favorite activities at Grams' house is to pretend. Taylor always decides the setting and casts the characters. If it's a castle, Taylor is queen. Grams is always relegated to some servant role. If it's an emergency room, Taylor is the doctor. Grams is the dying patient. One day Kaye said, "Taylor, today at pretend, how about I choose what we play and who plays what?"

Taylor reflected on this a while and said, "Okay, but I get to be the important one." Producers have strong leadership characteristics. Help them develop appropriate ways to move ahead of the crowd.

The best expression I've heard lately was from a Promoter mom. She has not one but two Producer children with a Peacekeeper in the middle. She said when she and the Peacekeeper would see the two Producers coming they would turn to one another and say, "Red alert, red alert!"

## GOOD NEWS/BAD NEWS

| Good News | Bad News |
|---|---|
| Independent | Aloof—often not a warm cuddly child |
| Resourceful | Watch your belongings—they take what they need to make something happen |
| Logical | Will argue until they wear you down |
| Determined | Bullheaded |
| Decisive | Opinionated |
| Witty | Sarcastic |
| Positive | All hot air |
| Global—big picture | Head in the clouds—unrealistic |

## PRODUCERS

| Teenage Producers | |
|---|---|
| Respected | Hold peers at arm's length |
| High profile | Selfish |
| Accomplished | Uses people to get places |
| Self-assured | Pompous/covers self-doubt |
| Dynamic | Callous/cold |
| Driven | Calculating |
| Forceful | Lacks people skills |
| Competitive | Win at all costs |
| Capable | Takes on too much |
| Type-A | Intense |
| Inventive | Ruthless |
| Competent | Intolerant |
| Leader/take charge | Controlling/challenge authority |

## ◯PATIENT PEACEKEEPERS/GREEN/OVALS

My neighbors, Robert and Armene, gave a clear picture of a Peacekeeper child when they talked about their daughter, Emily, who is definitely a Patient Peacekeeper. Armene said Emily was a caretaker from the moment she was mobile. She was always tender with animals, other babies, children, and her toys. Once school age, Emily was the friend of the underdog. Not wanting anyone to be excluded or left out, Emily turned their home into a haven for the lost and needy. According to her father, in her teen years she added the weird. Thanks to Emily and her kind heart, one of her projects stayed in their home a week and gave everyone head lice.

Robert recalls the time she brought home a litter of newborn kittens abandoned by their mother. For this act of love the whole family got ringworm. Robert shrugged his shoulders and said, "Emily's so kind and caring with the purest of motives. We couldn't get angry at her—even when we got ringworm. I have to be careful not to tell Emily I'm disappointed in her. It destroys her. She is the most compassionate and sensitive member of our family. In fact, sometimes she puts the rest of the family to shame because she really is her brother/sister's keeper, and the rest of us are busy focusing on ourselves. Emily is a gentle, tender-heart who really loves and cares about people."

I have watched Emily from birth to womanhood. She is a bright girl who approached school like she does life. She took school slowly and steadily, trying not to get stressed out anymore than absolutely necessary. She got the grades she needed to go to college.

She went to the college of her choice, graduated with good enough grades to get into the master's program of her choice, and worked as a corporate psychologist in a large company. Emily knows who she is and what she needs more than any young person I know.

One Christmas break she told me she was taking a semester off. She said, "I broke my own rules last semester. I tried to work and take too many classes. I got a huge case of the "whelms." Of course, I asked her to define "whelms."

She said, "I've always known I couldn't load my plate as much as Tim, my type-A driven brother. He likes life in the fast lane, taking on more than three people can handle. I don't. I like to take life steadily and practically. I like space and independence with little outside demand on me. It's important for me to keep my life manageable. Otherwise I get overwhelmed quickly. A bad case of overwhelmed becomes the 'whelms.' When I'm 'whelmed,' the peace and harmony I must have goes away, and I become passive, resistive, and apathetic. I drop out emotionally. I become too overwhelmed to function. That's where I am right now. So, I'm going to get off the merry-go-round, regroup, and try again in summer school."

Now, I'm watching Emily function in her role as wife and mother. I had coffee with her recently and listened to the update on her life. She said, "I don't like juggling too many balls at a time. I knew I did not want to be a working mother. So we sacrifice because I don't work, but it's worth it. I keep my life as peaceful and steady as I can, considering I have three young children. I've started a Mothers of Pre-Schoolers (MOPS) group. Being a stay-at-home mom can be lonely and isolating, and I would hate to think of other women in that place when there is companionship and support out there. Organizing this group is enough for me right now.

I'm learning to set good boundaries because I have such a high need to keep everyone happy and everything harmonious. If I didn't have good boundaries, people would walk all over me, and then I'd be an overwhelmed doormat."

As I drove home from my meeting with Emily I was thinking that this kind, considerate, needing-to-please child has grown into a woman who is gracious, diplomatic, and compassionate. Plus, she has a good understanding of her own strengths and limitation. How blessed her family is.

### Adults Need to Understand This about Patient Peacekeepers:

- We like a life that is as conflict free as possible.
- For emotional growth we need . . .
  - ☞ to have you understand our personality type.
  - ☞ to be accepted for who we are not what we do.
  - ☞ to have you to help us feel we have worth.
  - ☞ to have you understand that we have kind hearts.
  - ☞ respect.
  - ☞ independence.
- Our specialties are . . .
  - ☞ balance.
  - ☞ diplomacy.
  - ☞ staying calm, cool, collected.
  - ☞ being kind, nice, and easy to get along with.

☞ adaptability.

☞ being practical and having common sense.

☞ being pleasant.

☞ concerned for how others feel.

☞ cooperation.

- We feel sad when . . .

  ☞ people are angry.

  ☞ people fight.

  ☞ people are mean.

  ☞ no one helps us with mean people.

  ☞ we are blamed for something we didn't do.

  ☞ we are ignored.

  ☞ people are left out.

- We fear . . .

  ☞ things changing all the time.

  ☞ not being considered good people.

  ☞ too many things to do at once.

  ☞ problems.

  ☞ dealing with problems.

- We enjoy . . .

  ☞ family outings when everyone gets along.

  ☞ friends and family together when everyone gets along.

  ☞ working on something we like either alone or with a friend.

  ☞ parties where no one is left out.

☞ school when everyone is nice.

☞ teams sometimes—but with a coach that doesn't shout or exclude players.

■ Help us with . . .

☞ speaking up for ourselves.

☞ being too sensitive.

☞ being taken advantage of by more dominating people.

☞ joining in what is going on around us.

☞ not getting lost in the shuffle.

☞ being too kind and nice.

## ATTENTION GROWN-UPS: THIS IS IMPORTANT STUFF!

## WANTS AND NEEDS

### Status Quo

Peacekeepers don't want their boats of life rocking, tipping from side to side, and definitely not capsizing. They don't want to radically change courses either. They want to plot a slow but steady course and sail along in the tranquil waters of life.

When their boat of life is sailing along smoothly, it gives them time to experience the peace and harmony that they believe life is supposed to have.

Divorce or separation for these children violates this high need for status quo. These children usually don't act out; they withdraw. When, and if, they act out, it will come with a force that has a great deal of stored-up emotion behind it.

After I discussed the Peacekeeper child in one seminar, a mother told me this story:

I have two children, Zach, a Producer who's fourteen, and Kevin, a Peacekeeper who's twelve. I have been divorced for two years. The first year, Zach verbally bombarded me with accusations, criticisms, assertions, and an opinion about exactly how I should handle everything. Life with him was like living with a verbal machine gun—a constant ratta-tat-tat of words piercing my soul. Zach was brutal.

Kevin, who had always been a quiet, compliant child, became almost stoic. I knew it was not a good sign. Between my personal pain of having my husband leave me for another woman and my Producer son never shutting up, I pretty much let Kevin quietly drift that first year.

Zach was always huffing and puffing, like a strong, constant annoying wind of words. But Kevin was like a tornado, calm, until it blew through wiping everything out. One day in year two, Kevin blew. In one week he kicked a teacher's aide, ripped all the flowers out of my garden, and ran away from home for twenty-four hours before we found him.

At the end of the week the three of us started therapy. Kevin is learning how to express himself in appropriate ways, a little at a time, instead of keeping it in, then blowing. Zach is learning to be a little more compassionate and less judgmental and opinionated. I'm learning more about all three of us so we can meet each other's needs and start to enjoy life again.

I am a Promoter desperately wanting some fun to return to our lives.

## Independence

Peacekeepers can be very outgoing and social and also extremely content in solitary activities. These children report that they like to read, build models, do puzzles, and play with Legos. They also enjoy arts and crafts and computers. They enjoy a variety of quiet activities. For most of this green group, spending time alone in pursuit of something they enjoy is a very good thing.

Having friends and being a friend is very important, but these children can also stand apart from the crowd and be their own person. They know who they are, and most know what they want. Compliant by nature, Peacekeepers can be pushed only so far. When they take their independent stand it might look like stubbornness with a silent will of iron.

## Comfort

Of all the personality types, these Peacekeeper children have the highest need for comfort. Comfort in all forms—from their clothing to their food to their environment. If your green Peacekeeper child is having a bad day, remember you can comfort this child with favorite, familiar foods. This child will also respond positively to an ordered, quiet setting. Perhaps giving your child a backrub while he/she tells you about the upsets of the day will be just what this peaceful child needs to find balance again.

My friend Susan has a Peacekeeper son, Will. As a nursing infant, Will would reach for his mother's long hair and rub it on his face while feeding.

Susan learned that Will wanted soft sheets and blankets in his crib and later on his bed. He would, again, gently rub the fabric on his face as he went to sleep. When Will was distressed, Susan often found him in his room reading or listening to music but always with a soft blanket close at hand to rub. The ability to comfort themselves is a skill these green Peacekeeper children often learn early in life.

## GOOD NEWS/BAD NEWS

| Good News | Bad News |
| --- | --- |
| Compliant | Passive resistive |
| Diplomatic | Wishy-washy |
| Listens | Stoic |
| Kind | Smothering |
| Supportive | Uninvolved |
| Calm | Unenthusiastic |
| Steady | Overwhelmed |
| Patient | Indecisive |
| Malleable | Stubborn |

## PEACEKEEPERS

| Teenage Peacekeepers | |
|---|---|
| Concerned | Codependent |
| Creative dressers | Weird |
| Independent | Isolated/loner |
| Nonchalant | Lazy |
| Accommodating | Used by peers |
| Compassionate | Nonassertive |
| Slow-paced | Unmotivated |
| Individualists | Nonconforming |
| Caring | Apathetic |
| Balanced | Not motivated by what others think |

## PARENT ALERT

The Peacekeeper child in the classroom is sometimes invisible. They quietly sit, steadily doing the work, trying to fit in so they don't draw attention to themselves.

They don't make waves or get in trouble, and they definitely don't do anything to upset the teacher. In this present day with chaos in many classrooms, green Peacekeeper kids can be a joy, but they are often overlooked and slip through the cracks. *Parents, talk to the teachers to make sure they know your child is there and getting his or her needs met.*

# CHAPTER 12

# PARENTAL GUIDANCE ADVISED

> **TO THE ADULTS IN OUR LIVES:**
> Please read all this stuff below to *understand us.*

## PROMOTER PARENTS

Living life to the fullest and having fun while you're at it is important to Promoters. Many Promoters are just grown-up kids, so they are great at playing with their children. This relationship-oriented group enjoys big people and little people, socializing, and freedom. Energetic and spontaneous, these parents are usually involved in a variety of activities and events with their children. Life with a Promoter parent is anything but routine and boring.

Born encouragers and motivators, Promoter parents often serve as personal cheerleaders to their children and any other child who crosses their path. Most in this yellow Promoter group express a real love for children.

Some Promoter parents need to work on structure and follow through in the lives of their children. A fun-filled high adventure life may be good for the parent but not always the child.

## Perky Promoters

There usually is not lack of love in this relationship. Both are good at self-expression so communication is generally okay to great.

Lack of structure, no attention to details, and forgetfulness can plague this relationship. The Promoter adult will need to model materials and time management to these hang-loose kids. These children have creative minds flooded with an idea per minute. Organizing everything from thoughts to belongings and schoolwork can be challenging. Since both adults and children like a great deal of variety, focusing should be worked on in this relationship.

Managing relationships is usually easy for these children. Due to their "go for the gusto" attitude and love for people and life, they are usually popular with peers. Telephones ringing and friends coming and going are not uncommon if you have Promoter children. The adult Promoters should understand the social nature of Perky Promoters.

## Precise Planners

This parent-child relationship has less in common than more in common. These children want routines, structure, and order. These traits do not come naturally to most Promoters. Planner children like to be on time and follow a schedule. Late adults are upsetting to these children. Disorganization and unscheduled changes are difficult for these orderly kids to manage. Planner children want to get life right. Details and quality are important to them.

Planner children can be rather serious and no nonsense. Promoters are playful and casual. Help the Planner children in your life to find the light side of life. Some Promoter adults need to get their acts together in order to be more effective in the lives of Planner children.

## Powerful Producers

The shared traits of parents and children are in their enjoyment of adventure and some element of risk. Both are innovative possibility thinkers with strong verbal skills. Promoter parents love freedom and so do their Producer children. These parents need to give these children as much freedom as is reasonable and safe. In most cases these independent, determined, responsible children can handle appropriate responsibilities. Over advising and controlling will not work with these "I've got it together, get out of my way" children.

It is possible that these children may be more determined about the events of their lives than the parents. Producer children want to take on life in a big way. Leadership traits may show up early in these children. The flip side of being a strong dynamic leader is manipulation, domination, and over-controlling. Promoter parents have good people skills and should model win/win leadership for these bold children.

## Patient Peacekeepers

The commonality between these parents and children is their tender hearts and relationship skills. Both care about people and want to please others. Promoter parents with their high need for variety, action, and activities in their lives can overwhelm these slower-paced children. A word of advice to parents—give these green Peacekeeper children advance notice of changes in plans and schedules when possible. They need some processing time to adjust to change. Everyone will be happier if these children do not have to change courses abruptly.

These children are often contented, self-contained, and do not need life to be a three-ring circus. Most of these children prefer to take life in small steady steps, not quantum leaps.

Peacekeeper children are generally not as social as Promoters are. One or two quality friends are comfortable for them. They do not need a cast of thousands running in and out of their lives. Many relationships to manage can bring confusion and chaos to these keep-life-simple-and-calm children.

Peacekeeper children have a high need to please. Encouragement and affirmations go a long way with these children. Remember these children are about peace. Anger, rage, and ugliness make these children retreat inside themselves to avoid life when it is not about peace and harmony.

## PLANNER PARENTS

Traditional values of family, education, and often religion are important to this group. Most Planners are concerned with providing stability, security, and routine for their children. The Planners need for an orderly life filters down into their parenting.

Planners want their children to achieve *but* to achieve the right way. Process is very important for this personality type. These analytical, practical parents have plenty of suggestions for the right way to do things. Many parents in this group like to tell their children not only what to do but also how to do it.

Some are very narrow in their view of the right way. They place perfectionistic, unrealistic expectations on their children. Many Planner parents are guilt-ridden because of their eternal quest to get everything right and, of course, life is not perfect, so they experience some sense of failure and guilt. Planner parents often pass guilt down to their children. Some parents do it knowingly and others unknowingly.

Their Planner children can absorb this guilt because they, too, are plagued with trying to do life perfectly, and guilt can find a home in some of these children. The Promoter or Producer children who have Planner parents aren't as likely to absorb the guilt as their Planner siblings might.

### Perky Promoters

These free-spirit children do not care about systems and order because systems and order look like boundaries and containment. Many Promoter children are not good at managing materials and belongings. Something they own is always lost or missing. Many in this group are just plain messy.

The Planner parents and Promoter children are opposite in most ways. The Planner parent is task oriented, trying to get life right while the Promoter child is relationship oriented, wanting to live life and have fun.

Some Planner parents have an inflexible nature. Rigidity and details will not work with most Promoter children. Do not try to capture or contain these children with rigid rules and restrictive structure. They will spend all their time and energy trying to figure out how to get the freedom they want and need. The harder you squeeze, the more they will struggle to get free. Eventually this struggle will turn into rebellion.

These are possibility-thinking children with high energy. You want to work with them toward managing their own lives with as much freedom as is reasonably safe to give them. They have a playful nature, and you need to make the playgrounds of their lives safe but large enough that they can experience life in their expansive way.

The problem here is many of these children don't look like they have their acts together. Remember these are children who do not want their acts together—especially by Planner parent standards. They like winging it through life. Life must be an exciting adventure, and if you have parents with a detailed map, then where is the thrill?

Planner parents with their schedules and plans may become frustrated with these children. Remember these children are not like you, and their ways are *not* your ways. Motivating and encouraging with tons of verbal affirmations versus rigid rules and severe punishments works better with these children. As hard as it is going to be for you, the more space you can realistically give these social, energetic children—the more they will find their own flexible boundaries. These children will profit from logical consequences of stepping outside the boundaries you have set rather than from punishment.

## Precise Planners

The Planner parent can help Planner children establish systems and order in their lives. These children are trying to get things in life done right. Help them do it right. Some Planner children have perfectionistic tendencies. Do what you can as a parent to help them target and hit realistic goals. Even Planner parents with Planner children might find these children are more perfectionistic than their parents or vice versa. This can be a source of frustration.

Modeling options and alternate solutions to these children is important. Precise Planners take life seriously. As the adult you are responsible to bring lightness and encouragement to these no-nonsense children.

## Powerful Producers

These children are probably going to have a larger worldview and be more visionary than you are. They will achieve and accomplish but may be aiming for quantity first and quality later—if ever. You may frustrate them by giving too many specifics and details. These are big-picture children who like to lead and be in charge. Control can be an issue here. Planner parents need to guard against being nitpicky and appreciate that these children have a vision of the big picture, not the details that make up that picture.

These results-oriented children believe in doing what it takes to get the job done—the end justifies the means. Coaching and guiding these children usually works better than rigid rules and tight controls.

## Patient Peacekeepers

Planner parents will provide the stable systems and routine these green group children need. Warning to Planners: Some of these children will give "slow paced" new meaning. Allow time in your daily schedule for these children who sometimes move at a tortoise's pace because that's the pace they like. These are children who have no need to rush through life—strolling suits them perfectly. Giving your Peacekeeper children space and their own pace will eliminate lots of nagging and frustration for both of you.

Some Peacekeeper children can be stubborn and passive resistive. The more you nag, the deeper they dig in their heels, and neither of you is happy. As you respect their need for independence and pace, you will find these children more malleable and less stubborn.

Peacekeeper children are little tender-hearts who want right relationships. Tension and lack of harmony are hard on these children. Help them move through life with as much steadiness and balance as possible.

Note: regarding divorce and separations. Remembering that steadiness and predictability are key for Planner and Peacekeeper children, divorce is going to be particularly hard on these children. Divorce brings change. Divorce brings instability and disharmony. Peacekeeper children, who are going through life looking for relationships that work, are going to be particularly hard hit by any kind of domestic discord.

## PRODUCER PARENTS

Winning at the game of life is extremely important to Producers. Most Producer parents put pressure, seen and unseen, on their children to get their acts together, accomplish, and win. This attitude applies to school, sports, after school activities, and work. Many Producers are what has become popularly referred to as Type-A personalities. They are driven to be competent and successful.

This group tries to pass their attitudes and drive onto their children. Some of their Producer and Planner children will resonate with their task-oriented, driven parents. But often their Promoter and Peacekeeper children aren't running life as a race with goals and winning in mind. They are living life for the sheer joy of just experiencing it—win, lose, or draw. Producer parents need to realize not every person is as competitive, determined, and goal oriented as they are.

Being task oriented, Producer parents need to remember that raising a child is more about relationship than a task. Too many people in this red Producer group focus on the tasks involved with a child and forget to relate. Hugging and laughter might be valid goals for this week! Most Producer parents could lighten up a little—or a lot—depending on the personalities of their children.

### Perky Promoters

Most Promoter children are not as results oriented as their Producer parents. These children are free spirited. Do not try to capture or contain them in a too-small space. They will spend all their time and energy trying to figure out how to get the freedom they want and need.

These are possibilities-oriented children with high energy. You want to work with them not against them. They are playful by nature, and you need to make the playgrounds of their lives safe but large enough for them to do some discovering on their own.

Some Producers have a controlling nature. Rigidity and domination will not work with these Promoter children. The harder you squeeze, the more they will struggle to get free. Eventually this struggle will turn into rebellion.

The problem here is many of these children don't look like they have their act together. Remember that these children don't want their act together—especially by Producer parent standards. They like winging it through life. Life must be an exciting adventure. The thrill of the hunt is important to them. Producer adults are focusing on completion and winning. These children's main focus is the event itself. Finish would be good, winning would be good, also, but the process and the happening is the real thrill. Being there and making new friends along the way are important to Promoter children.

Producer parents and Producer adults, with their goals and targeted plans, may frustrate these children. Remember these children are not like you, and their ways are *not* your ways. You will need to give many more verbal affirmations to these children than you think they've earned. Encouraging these children is *not* about their earning it–it is about their needing it.

You need to stand beside them as a cheerleader with tons of "U can do" and "U are great" cheers.

## Precise Planners

These children want to achieve and accomplish just as you do. The difference is Producer parents often insist on telling the child what and how to achieve. Planners are masters at figuring out systems and procedures. Generally, these children are going to be more perfectionist than their parents. Planner children want to accomplish with quality while their Producer parents are more concerned about quantity.

Parents need to set the guidelines for the "whats" of their children's lives, but if they could give these children some latitude in the "hows" these children would probably do very well. In most cases they will find their children know how to do what the parents want. Parents need to find ways to let these children earn independence and freedom with the structures and processes of their lives.

## Powerful Producers

This is a battle of the wills. Both are strong. These children were born with a need to be in charge of life. Parents need to find ways to let these children earn independence and freedom. Remember these children value what you value—accomplishment, competency, and winning. Help them learn appropriate skills and attitudes to find achievement.

Producer children usually need guidelines and coaching, not rigidity and tight controls. Most Producer children are self-starters and need you by their side without pulling or pushing. Many of these children will put plenty of pressure on themselves—more from you may be too much!

***Note to Producer Fathers:*** If you have a Peacekeeper son, there is a good chance this child is not as competitive as you are. If you are into competitive sports, your son may not be into competitive sports or even individual sports. You may have a son, much to your dismay, who will never want to play football, tennis, or soccer. Your child may be interested in other things. If you have an individualist, try to find something that you both mutually enjoy. Support him in the things that interest him, and you enjoy the things that interest you. Pushing this passive child to be something he is not could be destructive in the long term.

## Patient Peacekeepers

These children are of a very different nature than their Producer parents and other Producer adults. These children are peacemakers and peacekeepers. They will go far out of their way to avoid conflicts and scenes. Family discord is extremely hard on these children. They are kind, gentle children. Peacekeepers may or may not be driven to accomplish, but if there is a drive for something, they will quietly and independently go after what they want. This parent/child combination has different action styles.

Control is an issue. These children want a life that is independent. They don't want to control anyone and resent being controlled by others. Guidance that is fair and appropriate they understand and accept. They want their space and do not like confrontation, domination, or forcefulness. These children will say "Yes" to keep the peace but will often not do what they said they would do. They can be stubborn and passive resistive.

Peacekeepers are compliant. They lead life with their hearts and can be gentle—but do not mistake this for weakness. They have a silent will of iron, which you do not want to have to confront. Understand and work with them. Do not try to control them.

Producer parents need to understand and respect these children for who they are and how different they are from themselves. Most of these children do better with softer parenting skills. These children want to please and avoid conflict. Don't push them. Rather take their hands and walk beside them with gentleness.

Give these children advance notice of changes in plans and schedule when possible. They need some processing time to adjust to change. Everyone will be happier if this child does not have to change courses abruptly.

This child may not ever want to achieve in the way you do. Being a good human being is more important to these children than being a good human doing!

## PEACEKEEPER PARENTS

These are the parents with heart. This green group brings balance, fairness, and a strong sense of what others are feeling to parenting. Peacekeepers like life to be balanced and calm. However, their "don't rock the boat" motto forgot to include children! Children, by their very nature, bring situations that rock the boat. Most Peacekeepers have the ability to float above the craziness of parenting. They stay calm, cool, and collected come what may.

Peacekeeper parents promote harmony in the family. They are good listeners, using their strong negotiating skills to bring peace to the "did not" and "did so" of sibling rivalry.

They are accepting and sometimes too gentle. These parents error frequently on the side of leniency. Because they do not like to be forced into activities or behaviors, neither are they comfortable forcing their children into activities and behaviors that the children resist. So an internal struggle for many Peacekeeper parents is knowing how much pushing is productive and when is pushing too much. However, these patient parents can "lay down the law" when they need to.

### Perky Promoters

The parents and these children both make their decisions with their hearts. People, relationships, values, and feelings are commonalties for this combination. They are both people-persons. Friendliness, caring, acceptance, and a good nature are characteristics of both personalities.

The Promoter children want more going on in life than Peacekeepers usually do. These freewheeling, activity-a-minute children do not want a steady, status quo life like their parents. Life with Promoter children can feel busy and chaotic. Many Promoter children seem to need help with structure, attention to details, and forgetfulness. These children are moving fast down the road of life and have little time for organization. Their creative minds are flooded with an idea a minute.

Organizing everything from thoughts to belongings and schoolwork can be challenging for these children. The Peacekeeper parent will need to teach these children time management skills. Peacekeeper parents know how to focus and stick with a project—usually their Promoter children do not. Teach them, but don't do it for them.

These are rock-your-boat children. Due to their "go for the gusto" attitude and love for people and life, these children are often popular. Promoter children enjoy life. These Pied Piper children welcome friends, friends, and more friends. Telephones ringing and friends coming and going are all part of the Promoter children's lives. Peacekeeper adults—just take a motion sickness pill and enjoy the scenery.

**Precise Planners**

The similarities this parent/child combination enjoys are their practical outlook on life, a desire for a life that is steady and planned, and compliance with rules.

Some Planner children may want more structure and details in their lives than their parents do. These are children who like routine, schedules, and knowing what's going to happen next. The Peacekeeper parents may have to stretch to provide the systems and order in life that their children need.

Some Planner children may have perfectionist tendencies. Help them set realistic goals for themselves that they can achieve. These children usually want to be good students and get good grades. They manage their time and materials well. The structure of the education process fills these children's need for systems and order. Because of these children's need for predictability they do not like change. Moving, changes to the family, and divorce are very difficult for the children in the blue group.

## Powerful Producers

These children have a very different nature than their Peacekeeper parents. While the parents like life in the middle to slow lanes, the kids live in the fast lane. These are strong-willed children. Powerful Producers are determined, often demanding, self-pleasing, and ready to run the world.

Producer children are born wanting to be in charge of life. Remember, these children value independence as much or more than their Peacekeeper parents. Parents need to find ways to let these children earn independence and freedom. Help them to learn appropriate skills and attitudes to achieve this.

These children usually need guidelines and coaching—not rigidity and tight controls. Most Producer children are self-starters. Frankly, since you are not forceful in your parenting style, let these self-starters go longer and push harder than you would most likely prefer them to. Your supporting nature can complement their desire to accomplish. Just be careful not to diminish it. Many of these children will put plenty of pressure on themselves to achieve and succeed. Help them to be nice to themselves. Peacekeeper parents, be ready to enjoy a fast bumpy ride!

Help these children learn tenderness toward the human race. They are logic based while you are emotional based. You may need to give special teaching to the areas of people skills and TLC.

## Patient Peacekeepers

These parents understand these children's nature. They are both low-key and even-tempered. They both try to go through life doing their own thing.

Peacekeeper children want to please. Pleasing looks like keeping the peace. These harmony-driven children are all for a calm, stable environment.

Many children in this green group are self-contained and not demanding. They are sometimes the kids who slip through the cracks in large groups like classrooms and youth groups. But Peacekeeper parents know this about their children, and most are watching. Peacekeeper adults prefer to ignore conflict situations, but they need to speak up and be advocates for these children.

These children prefer a single project at a time and like to set their own pace and work independently or with a friend. Parents need to help them not to be overwhelmed by the demands of life. Many children in this group are easily overwhelmed with too many demands placed on their time. They like steady, status quo situations with minimal amounts of change. A word of advice to parents—give these children advance notice of changes in plans and schedules when possible. They need some processing time to adjust to change. Change is not their favorite thing.

These children enjoy being part of a team that is accepting and supporting. Because of their sense of fairness and fair play they may not be highly competitive.

# CHAPTER 13

# SO WHAT'S THE PLAN?

The key family action plan is to start spending more time together. Everyone meets at the kitchen or dining room table and nobody brings an electronic or battery-operated piece of equipment. The television is also off. They come, hands and hearts free if you're blessed. If the heart part isn't there yet, remember to start with what you can manage. No gadgets, you do have control of the hands-free part. For this action plan dinner, you might want to make it fun like our friends Peter and Mary do. It's a backwards dinner and you eat a small dessert first followed by dinner.

Then Mom or Dad, whoever read this book, or both in the best-case scenario, explains the plan. Discuss with your mate ahead of time about the family action plan and the outcomes you desire. A positive result would be everyone knowing their own personality type and the types of the rest of the family. This is extremely key to the success of the plan, the future evenings, and the rest of your lives. On my website at www.Peopleskills4u.com are personality type surveys for the whole family, starting with children kindergarten age through teens, and an adult Personality Type Indicator that you can order. If you don't want to order these indicators, then use the suggestions below.

The plan has to be age appropriate so let's start with younger children, say around age five. If they can't read, it has to be verbal. Keep it real simple. Use these words to represent the four personality types:

- **Friendly (Promoter)**

- **Dependable (Planner)**

- **Likes to be in charge (Producer)**

- **Kind (Peacekeeper)**

So the lead parent asks the child or children, "Here are four descriptions; which one describes you the **best**?" Let them take turns. If the children or a child has trouble choosing at first, then you use yourself as an example. Tell the family which of the descriptions you would pick for yourself and explain why you think what you picked best describes you. Ask your mate if the choice you picked best describes you and ask him or her to give an example. Ask the children if they agree if that choice is the best pick for you. If the children catch on, repeat the description; if not, have your mate select the description that best applies to him or her and repeat the process. If a child is still having trouble, you might ask if you could suggest what word or words you think best describes the person. If the child agrees, do so. The other members of the family could contribute to your comments also.

This exercise works better if the words are written on cards or paper. If some children can read and some can't, write it anyway. The ones who can't read will catch on and maybe learn to read a word as a side benefit. Each evening pick four different words and ask each family member to choose. Give this book to older children and let them bring a word or words from each personality type. Always use the strength words and not the blind spot words. Families need to affirm and not diminish. The diminishing will creep in but try to keep it positive.

Try not to tell family members what you think their personality types are. Let them figure it out on their own.

If they can read, guide them to the four different charts in the children section. Have them read each chart. Most kids will figure it out.

If they can't decide what type they are, start with having them choose the personality type that is the least like them and work to the most.

Eventually your family will have a valuable communication tool. If the children in your family understand themselves better, and their siblings and their parents do also, your family will be well on its way to having better communication and hopefully less conflict. Remember it's the difference in our personality types that trip us up. So making sure each family member knows the personality traits in the other family members will make all the difference to strong family relationships.

*I work with a guy I won't name.*
*He can't get his head in the game.*
*I am frequently annoyed!*
*Why was he employed?*
*Could he about me feel the same?*

# COWORKERS

*The Workplace*

In my years as a team building consultant, I was never contacted to work with a smooth-running, mutual and neutral, high-functioning team. No, I got the infighting, backstabbing, poorly led groups, with dirty motives. The bad news for business and the good news for my company is that there are a lot of infighting kinds of groups out there. Companies, with their leadership, management, departments, and teams, all have the same relationship problems. It is not that the job, project, or task is too complicated or impossible to solve; it's never about the tasks. It's always about the people. If you've got people, you've got problems.

My history shows if you add a strong foundation for understanding personality types, it leads to a better understanding of coworkers, and an increase in trust—which is a must in every relationship. If you are able to apply this, you would achieve respect and, at the very least, tolerance. A team, division, or project group that understands personality types and speaks each other's personality language to the best of each individual's ability, and with mutual admiration and respect, can tackle and achieve anything the company assigns them.

How is this done? Start with the basics. Know what each personality type brings to the team. Divide the work as effectively as possible based on core personality strengths, education, knowledge, skills, and experience with the task at hand. Also part of this formula for team success is the leader and his or her leadership style, attitude, and people skills. If the leader has it together and works with and watches for dissension, negative attitudes, and low morale, and immediately addresses them, then the team has a good chance of being one we would all like to join.

One of my favorite success stories is of a young engineer with a Fortune 500 company. As a solo act he'd been a rising star in the company galaxy. But managing people turned out not to be part of his skill set. Truthfully someone above him had made a mistake in promoting him to this position. He was too young and inexperienced, with zero management training. On top of that the team had some basic foundation problems. This young man had less seniority than three-fourths of the team. Seniority was a high value in this particular company.

A company store mentality permeated the whole corporate culture. As one of the state's largest employers, it was a big deal to work for this company, and how long one worked there was a key value. So Young Buck, as the senior members of the team called him behind his back, was already behind the eight ball from day one. Add to this the fact that three members of this team each believed they should have had the promotion to his position. Outrage doesn't begin to describe it. The Fearsome Three led the backstabbing and sabotaging. A well-constructed plan for Young Buck's career demise was solidly in place as I held my first team building session with his new team.

The good news for the team and me was that this young man had natural leadership ability buried in his youthful heart and soul. He basically was a diamond in the rough. He was humble. He knew that he didn't know, but was willing to learn. This is always a huge key factor in leadership and team transformation.

He was bold and didn't mind consulting the consultant. I got plenty of phone calls at my office. He said in one of his first calls, "I want to know everything you know about personality types. I learned how to be an engineer and now I'll learn how to manage other engineers."

We strategized on the phone for hours, everything from group meetings to individual conversations. He was bright, a quick study, absorbed information like a sponge, and had a charming authenticity about him that made me a fan. The way he learned to understand and meet the needs of his team in record time made us both look good.

He also had two very lucky breaks come his way. Two of the three arch enemies on his team got opportunities to move ahead in the company and left his team. Enemy number three decided to take early retirement. But he still had some very senior people on his team whom he won over with his newfound people skills.

This young man's People Skills Series Personality Type Indicator scores were highest in Producer red, making him a natural leader. But the thing that was his personal key success factor for overcoming the leadership situation he'd been placed in was that his secondary type was actually a tie between Planner blue and Promoter yellow. In high school, college, and early career it was his Producer and Planner strengths that got him near the top as he pursued his engineering profession. Getting an education, then a job, then succeeding at the job had been mostly about tasking. Management required a new skill set.

After the first day of training with his team when everyone else had gone home for the day, he said, "I know what I have to do to be a successful leader."

I asked, "What?"

He held up his indicator and tapped his finger on the Promoter yellow column and said, "I've never been encouraged to develop this part of my personality. My parents are Planners. I'm an only child born to older no-nonsense parents." He chuckled. "In fact Dad taught engineering at M.I.T. and my mother's a high school math teacher whose favorite saying is, *A place for everything and everything in its place.*"

I agreed, "Doesn't get much bluer than that."

Then he thumbed through the training manual I had prepared for his team, stopping about five pages in and stated, "I need to develop the Promoter part of my personality because that's where I'm going to get the relationship skills and heart to work with my team. I've got the logic and tasking skills, now I need people skills."

Smiling, I said, "That's exactly right. After meeting with you twice and watching you today, I believe you can do it and, as a Promoter with the gift of encouragement, I'm cheering for you."

We have kept in touch over the years. When he started his own engineering firm at age thirty-eight, one of his first orders of business was having me certify his human resources department to train all the employees in the People Skills Series. To this day outside the door or on the desk of each of the individuals on his team is a small chart with the four personality T-shirt logos placed in the order of that person's personality type, high to lowest. His engineering company has been voted best company to work for several times at both the local and state level.

Teams I work with are as diverse in how they are formed as are the members themselves. I've had teams that were put together on behavior-based hiring. Sounded great in theory but lost something in the human melting pot of work. I've coached groups or teams that just happened through attritions and additions, your basic no-rhyme-or-reason team—or teams formed out of whatever organizational development trend was happening at the time; merged teams, default departments, stragglers, and shoved-alones banding together out of necessity. I've worked with them all. But the common denominator was that each team was average or below in performance usually because they lacked understanding and were poorly led. However they got together could not be my concern; it was how they would get along in the future that was my challenge.

What made a team, department, or group that was performing poorly move up the effective ladder? First, it was understanding and using the personality types, which promoted trust, acceptance, and respect for fellow team members. Other key success factors like team maturity, not in years but attitude, add to team effectiveness. Knowledge of the job, clearly defined goals, belief in the company and its leadership, and general good work ethics are some key components of teams that increase performance measurably. Of course, you can never minimize the importance of the leadership role.

As a team building consultant I have walked down a lot of corporate hallways. One day I observed a man who looked like an executive type sticking his head in and out of a row of empty office doors. I just walked pass but was curious because he had a sense of urgency about him. Finally, someone asked him, "What are you doing?"

He gave a response I will never forget and now often ask myself. He said, "I'm looking for the normal people."

Who are the normal people? Dictionary.com defines normal people as, "Approximately average in any psychological trait, such as intelligence, personality, or emotional adjustment." Psychobabble aside, I think my friend Patsy Clairmont sums it up well in the title of one of her books, *Normal Is Just a Setting on the Dryer*. We have all worked with some people who march to the beat of a different drum. There are a multitude of reasons someone does not fit within the boundaries of whatever a company has defined as their norm or normal people.

Frequently Human Resource managers want help with a team leader they believe would eventually have to go. I've had more than one HR VP say, "Do your best with this person in improving the way he/she leads the team. But basically you are part of our attempt to rehabilitate him/her in the best case scenario. In the worst case, having all this special coaching and then still having them fail will help our case if he/she files a grievance as a result of termination."

One of my early team building contracts was with a large Fortune 100 company. The Human Resources department suspected something I was to specify and confirm months into working with this team. With this particular contract, HR staff felt I was part of what the military calls CYA. Members of the department knew that in this case they better go by the book— and beyond. Hiring my company to work with this team, especially the leader, was part of the "beyond." Right here I would love to be able to say this story ended with the leader miraculously transformed and the team living happily ever after. As it turned out, this guy was using cocaine at a time when it was not a household word. He had to have been a frontrunner in the business world of this horrible addiction. When substance abuse is involved, a different kind of coaching is needed. The man was eventually terminated. One of his team members replaced him and wrote in a thank you letter some months later, "When I was promoted to team leader out of the chaotic Joe situation, I vowed I would use all the personality concepts you taught us. I have really tried. I believe it is working and the feedback from my team is that they feel understood for the first time in their working careers."

Understanding personality types works for "normal" people. Knowing strengths, blind spots, wants, needs and communication styles, plus a commitment to the team and each individual member, has been game changing in team after team. Understanding personality types can add value to any team, work group, or committee. But this information, and the techniques that flow from it, cannot overcome drug or alcohol abuse, mental illness or even the presence of extreme pain or chronic illness, especially in team leaders. These afflictions in most cases change behavior and muddy the waters of a person's personality.

# CHAPTER 14

# SOLUTIONS TO PEOPLE PROBLEMS

Understanding and respect are the two biggest deterrents to conflict. When you understand other workers' personality types you will have a leg up the proverbial ladder. Whether a construction ladder or corporate ladder, there are many workers and few leaders. Let's talk about the largest group first—the individual worker and what he or she brings to the workplace.

The task at work is to relate.

The Real YOU

## UNDERSTANDING PERSONALITY CHARACTERISTICS IN THE WORKPLACE

| Yellow Promoter | Blue Planner |
|---|---|
| Articulate, motivator | Organized, reliable, loyal |
| Energetic, enthusiastic | Scheduled, cautious |
| Optimistic, encourager | Deep thinker, conscientious |
| Flexible, fun, good networker | Logical, develops systems |
| Thinks out of the box, creative, brain storming | Maintains order, provides quality control |
| People specialist | Thoughtful, problem solver |
| Multitasking, possibilities oriented | Detailed record keeper, practical oriented |
| Promoters are usually good in sales and in jobs that require interaction. People gravitate to their positive energy and charismatic personality. Promoters are usually popular people magnets. | Planners are dependable, foundational people. They develop the systems, maintain them, and solve problems. Planners are solid citizens you can count on. |
| Red Producer | Green Peacekeeper |
| Leader, achiever, visionary, decisive | Diplomatic, seeks solutions |
| Driven, confident, competent, focused on the bottom line. | Good listener, steady, calm, balanced |
| Influential, results oriented | Adaptive |
| Productive, problem solver | Relationship oriented |
| Like challenges | Brings clarity, can stay mutual and neutral |
| Strong willed | Patient, kind, moderate, fair |
| Possibilities oriented | Practical oriented |
| Producers are great in a crisis, good at delegation and seeing the big picture. They are comfortable in leadership roles. Expediency is key to them. | Peacekeepers bring balance and harmony to the working environment. They are gentle giants who are well liked. They keep calm in a crisis. They excel in jobs that require counseling or service. |

**FYI**—If you are currently in a job search, be sure you work each of the strengths of your personality type into your story and on your resume. If your top two personality types are close in your number score, work the traits of both into your interviewing process. Remember you own these strengths and every company needs your strengths. So promote them! Also check the list of strengths for the four personality types in leadership in this section. There might be something there you can use. Blessings on your search.

## MUST KNOW

| Yellow Promoter | Blue Planner |
|---|---|
| 19% of total population | 35% of total population |
| Female 65%—male 35% | Male 60%—female 40% |
| Heart makes decision—emotion based | Brain makes decision—logic based |
| Direct communicator— tells vs. asks | Indirect communicator— asks vs. tells |
| Prefers relationships over tasks | Prefers tasks over relating with others |
| More extroverts than introverts | Close split/extroverts and introverts |
| Seeks change | Avoids change |
| **Red Producer** | **Green Peacekeeper** |
| 14% of total population | 32% of total population |
| Male 60%—female 40% | Female 65%—male 35% |
| Brain makes decision—logic based | Heart makes decision—emotion based |
| Direct communicator— tells vs. asks | Indirect communicator— asks vs. tells |
| Prefers tasks over relating with others | Prefers relationships over tasks |
| More extroverts than introverts | Close split/extroverts and introverts |
| Seeks change | Avoids change |

This chart was in the Family section and the Marriage section, but it's just as vital in the Coworker section.

## TASK AND RELATIONSHIP ORIENTATION

Task and relationship orientation is one of the most important components to know about your personality type. It is key both in your work environment and personal life. As the next chart indicates, Planners and Producers are task oriented while Promoters and Peacekeepers are relationship oriented.

Can Planners and Producers relate successfully with people? Of course, but some have to work harder at it than others. They know how to make it happen and get the job done because tasking is their comfort zone. Can Promoters and Peacekeepers task? Of course, but they'd rather relate because they understand people and relating to others is their specialty. They really are the people's pal. All personality types know it takes both tasking and relationship to complete any job effectively. Some are just better at doing both than others.

A training session for a large nationwide staffing placement agency drove this point home for all the participants. Here is an industry that must both task and relate. The task/relating components—acquiring clients, securing job orders, and finding the people to fill those jobs require both task and relationship. During the training, we looked at the components of their work in terms of which were task and which were relationship focused.

**Relationship components:** Selling a potential business client on using your placement firm takes relationship building. Interviewing potential candidates and making accurate decisions on who would fit, also takes relationship. Finding that right person to fit the job requires good people skills. Making the connection happen between the client and the candidate takes both task and relationship, but at this stage it's more relationship. Follow-up after the interview with both future employer and employee is also relationship in that more talk, interaction, and dialogue are required to negotiate the terms of the assignment.

**Task components:** Posting job orders, scheduling interviews with clients and candidates, recording candidate / employee data, and submitting invoices are all tasks important to getting the job done well. Tasking versus talking sums up this component.

After reviewing the general categories of their jobs, I gave them an assignment. The assignment was to meet in their top-scoring personality type group. So Promoters met in one office, Planners another, and so on. Each group was to decide and list which part of the job they liked best and answer this key question: *At the end of the working day when you are tired, what are your Actions and what are your Avoids?*

The feedback the participants gave me after the training was *what a relief it was to better understand themselves and why certain parts of the job energized and certain parts drained them. Each group had their "Aha" moments.*

Below is the feedback from the four personality type groups:

**Promoters** like the talking, meeting, interviewing, selling on the phone and in person the best. They love encouraging the candidates on how to interview, get the job and enjoy reassuring the employers that the right person is being sent their way. Data entry and research are the bane of their existence.

- At the ended of day—**RELATE**

- *The Action*—call a candidate or the client to see how the interview went.

- *The Avoids*—put off the record keeping.

**Planners** like the research and data part, keeping the systems in order, dotting their *i*'s, crossing their *t*'s, but keeping meetings and people interaction to a minimum. Because all that human interaction is draining.

- At the end of day—**TASK**

- *The Actions*—they logged all their data.

- *The Avoids*—making the follow-up calls. Putting them off until tomorrow when they are fresh and have more energy.

**Producers** like the end result . . . a placement. They know it takes both tasking and relating to make this happen. They like to keep the sales calls and candidate interviews to bottom-line effectiveness, with no excessive talking. They do not like tedious data entry but understand the value of records and data.

- At the end of day—**TASK**

- *The Actions*—make a list of potential new clients to contact tomorrow.

■ *The Avoids*—social dialogue with anyone.

**Peacekeepers** like the human interaction with both clients and candidates. They are thrilled when a position is filled to everyone's satisfaction. Copious record keeping is stressful and overwhelming. They dislike the data driven part of the job.

■ At the end of day—**RELATE**

■ *The Actions*—they make a follow-up call, relate to and encourage their client or candidate.

■ *The Avoids*—the data entry and reports.

When you are tired at the end of the day, try to work in your comfort area. It helps restore your energy.

| Task Oriented PLANNER | Task Oriented PRODUCER |
|---|---|
| Work Orientations: Thinking/ problem solving | Work Orientations: Moving people into action |
| Time Orientation: Past | Time Orientation: Present/future |
| Work Contributions: Planning, organizing | Work Contributions: Gets tasks done |
| Abilities: Works with existing and finished conditions by evaluating and adding quality. | Abilities: Influences the environment by overcoming obstacles to get immediate results. |
| Style: Formal and structured | Style: Formal and structured |
| Relationship Oriented PEACEKEEPER | Relationship Oriented PROMOTER |
| Work Orientations: Communicate, listen | Work Orientations: Motivate, build morale |
| Time Orientation: Immediate | Time Orientation: Present/future |
| Work Contributions: Diplomacy, solution seeker | Work Contributions: Intuition, ideas |
| Abilities: Collaborates with others. Makes sure people are included and feel good about the process. | Abilities: Enriches the environment by generating enthusiasm for action. Becomes the cheerleader. |
| Style: Informal, relaxed, warm | Style: Informal, relaxed, fun |

## CONNECTING AND COMMUNICATING WITH THE FOUR TYPES

A positive action step for good interaction and communication is to know your personality type and the type of others. All your work and personal interactions will be enriched when you try to communicate with an understanding of type. The following guidelines are in a business context but can also be applied to family and friends. Keep in mind Promoters and Producers are direct communicators, frequently making statements versus asking questions. Planners and Peacekeepers often ask questions to connect and communicate in a more indirect manner. Consider the strategies below when customizing your communication to the following types:

## CUSTOMIZED COMMUNICATING

### Customized Communicating: Yellow Promoter

- Be personable and friendly.
- Get to know the person before getting down to business.
- Don't hurry the discussion.
- Be entertaining and fast moving.
- Encourage brainstorming, ideas, opinions, and possibilities.
- Show how the idea is valuable to people and how it will affect people.
- Encourage dreams. Don't burst the bubble—encourage imagination.
- Don't give lots of details unless asked to do so.
- Show the aspects that are not routine.
- Keep it casual.
- Remember, they are direct communicators who are relationship oriented and feelings based.

## Customized Communicating: Blue Planner

- Be focused and organized.
- State facts, not opinions or beliefs.
- Put it in writing.
- Be systematic in your presentation.
- Be practical and realistic; document successful application.
- Show how your suggestion is a continuation of what is, not radical change.
- List pros and cons of each alternative.
- Focus on low risks.
- Be calm and reasonable.
- Present emotions and feelings as facts to be weighed in the decision.
- Allow time for analysis.
- Remember, they are indirect communicators who are task oriented and logic based.

## Customized Communicating: Red Producer

- Keep your relationship businesslike.
- Focus on goals and objective.
- Be direct.
- Be brief, concise, and organized.
- Be logical and do not ramble.
- Be intellectually critical and objective.
- Be confident and competent.
- Don't give lots of details unless asked to do so.
- List the pros and cons of each alternative.
- Tell them where they fit in-their opportunity.
- Argue facts, not personal feelings.
- Speak at a relatively fast pace.
- Remember, they are direct communicators who are task oriented and logic based.

## Customized Communicating: Green Peacekeeper

- Give them time to build trust in you.
- Get to know the person before getting down to business.
- Be personal and friendly.
- Be supportive of their feelings.
- Show how they can help.
- Make sure you understand their needs.
- Be informal.
- Maintain a relaxed steady pace.
- Be orderly. Show the steps involved.
- Be practical and realistic.
- Be aware that they may have difficulty being critical and giving negative feedback.
- Remember, they are indirect communicators who are relationship oriented and feelings based.

# CHAPTER 15

# LEADERSHIP AND PERSONALITY TYPE

The Personality Type Leadership Traits charts on the next pages are a collective effort. The credit goes to managers, project managers, group leaders, and division leaders who have been in my seminars. They were recorded by teams or individuals who were assigned to come up with the strengths and blind spots of each of the four types in leadership.

Over the years they have been amazingly similar. Please note, that what is perceived as strength is also in some cases perceived as a blind spot. Our strengths, sometimes taken too far, tend to blind or impede us. On the following pages are the strengths and blind spots for each of the four personality types in leadership.

# PERSONALITY TYPE LEADERSHIP TRAITS

| Promoter Strengths | Promoter Blind Spots |
|---|---|
| Charismatic | No attention to details |
| Charming | Smoozer–too social |
| Fun | Lies / Exaggerates |
| Encouraging | Has favorites |
| Warm | Late |
| Inventive | Lacks systems and order |
| Brainstormer | Changes mind frequently |
| Relational | Forgetful |
| Willing to engage | Unfocused |
| Cheerleader | Easily sidetracked |
| Inspirational | Impulsive |
| Influencing | Goes for relational event over the task |
| Articulate | |
| Visionary | Paperwork is messy / has mistakes |
| Thinks out of box | |
| Embraces change | Creates chaos |
| Flexible | Hyper / Loud / Interruptive |
| High energy | Might "best deal" you |
| Possibilities oriented | Goes back on word |
| Optimistic | Fickle |
| Well connected | Talks too much |
| *If you need your day brightened . . . take them to lunch.* | *Don't give them the original of anything.* |

## PERSONALITY TYPE LEADERSHIP TRAITS

| Planner Strengths | Planner Blind Spots |
|---|---|
| Honest | Analysis-paralysis |
| Integrity | Critical / Nit picky |
| Dependable | Rigid |
| Systematic | Too authoritative |
| Organized | Cold |
| Reliable | No people skills |
| Responsible | Militant |
| Fair and just | Anal retentive |
| Loyal | Negative |
| Thoughtful | Untrusting / Overly sensitive |
| Structured | Can't delegate |
| Practical | Can't see big picture |
| Problem-solver | Lives in past |
| Carries their part of the load | Narrow minded |
| Thinker | Poor communicator |
| Often right | Rather task than relate |
| Conforming | Too detailed |
| Cognitive | Perfectionist |
| Cautious | Boring |
| *Provides an orderly and organized environment.* | *Don't ask the time; they will tell you how to make a watch.* |

## PERSONALITY TYPE LEADERSHIP TRAITS

| Producer Strengths | Producer Blind Spots |
|---|---|
| Natural leader<br>Driven<br>Visionary<br>Determined<br>Achiever<br>Competent<br>Sharp<br>Bold<br>Forthright<br>Confident<br>Influential<br>Decisive<br>Possibilities oriented<br>Optimist<br>Thinks out of box<br>Efficient<br>Makes it happen | Arrogant<br>Domineering / Bulldozing<br>Manipulative<br>Too authoritative<br>Unemotional<br>Combative<br>Self-centered<br>Self-righteous<br>Egotistical<br>Judgmental<br>Controlling<br>Inflexible<br>Opinionated<br>Underhanded<br>Conniving<br>Cunning<br>Bossy, Rude / Insensitive |
| *If you want to win, get on their team.* | *This can be a poster person for toxic boss.* |

## PERSONALITY TYPE LEADERSHIP TRAITS

| Peacekeeper Strengths | Peacekeeper Blind Spots |
|---|---|
| Diplomatic<br>Kind<br>Fair<br>Relational<br>Listener<br>Mutual/neutral<br>Patient<br>Adaptive<br>Moderate<br>Collaborative<br>Seeks solutions<br>Seeks clarity<br>Stable<br>Accepting<br>Balanced<br>Practical<br>Harmonious | Indecisive<br>Pleaser<br>Overwhelmed<br>Too contemplative<br>Keeps options open too long<br>Stubborn / Passive resistive<br>Lazy / Unmotivated<br>Procrastinates<br>No sense of urgency<br>Stoically silent<br>Disengaged<br>Detached<br>Won't confront<br>Won't speak out<br>Wishy-washy<br>Selfish<br>Takes easy way out |
| *This is a heart-filled humanitarian.* | *Take a stand and move forward.* |

A word about blind spots, or as some might call them—weaknesses: these are usually our strengths taken too far. As an example, Promoters are usually articulate and good spokespersons but taken to extremes they just talk too much. The term "sit down and shut up" was probably first used on a Promoter. When a Planners' ability to analyze goes too far, they become imprisoned or paralyzed in information. Producers' ability to take charge, used to the extreme, is bossy and controlling. A Peacekeeper's need for kindness and compassion can also make them unable to assert themselves or confront when necessary. They can be perceived as weak pushovers.

The answer to these personal blind spots is self-awareness. When are you taking your strengths to excess? Watch yourself and realize when and how you take your strengths too far. Especially watch for situations that you find stressful. Adverse or stress-filled atmospheres tend to push us toward our blind spots.

## TOXIC BOSSES

A leader who enhances his or her strengths and diminishes his or her blind spots is going to be efficient and effective and usually good to work for. In the ten years I spent teaching a variety of classes at University of California at Irvine, all with a career focus, most of my students were returning graduates who were refocusing, reinventing themselves, or re-entering the workforce.

The stories of dysfunctional bosses and sick work environments far outweighed the stories of harmony. From sabotaging coworkers to toxic bosses, if you listened to my students' stories you would know it's harsh out there. An astounding number had quit perfectly good jobs within their training and skills sets because of a coworker or boss. I heard the same stories from different students every semester.

I think the most shocking work story came from a woman in my Advanced Career Exploration class. The make-up of that class was interesting with a mix of very bright, well-qualified people who were currently unemployed, reinventing themselves, or unfulfilled in their current jobs. There were several women with Master's degrees re-entering after child rearing. There was even a rocket scientist. The one thing they all had in common was the allure of a six-figure salary. This particular woman was about forty, sharp, articulate, savvy, and had a Master's in finance from Princeton. Taking her turn in the *Introducing Self* segment of the first class she said, "I'm using the wise adage 'get the next job from the desk that you are currently occupying.' I have what many would call a fabulous job but I am here so that I can plan a wise and well-thought-out exit strategy."

That caught the whole group's attention. She went on, "I will not reveal the name of my company but they are a Fortune 500 company. I have embossed business cards with a prestigious title and a job that is challenging enough to keep me learning, but one I can do without a great deal of stress. I don't have to travel and I make over six figures." At this point her fellow students gave a collective gasp.

She acknowledged their reaction. "I know, I get your negative reaction or worse whenever I share my story. But what is the one part of my job I didn't mention?"

An older male class member in the back said knowingly, "The boss from hell!"

She smiled for the first time since standing. "You are exactly right. Toxic doesn't even begin to describe this guy. And please, before you start throwing suggestions like transfers, placating, ignoring, and getting thicker skin, let me just say, I've tried anything you can think of and more. Money is not worth the stress this man is putting on my soul and body. I live on migraine medicine and antacid tablets."

During my tenure at the university, because of my students' stories I could write a complete chapter on toxic bosses. In the first year I promised my students, who had worked for a plethora of bosses that ranged from toxic to weak and ineffective, that I would note their stories and keep a list of what each of the four personality type bosses could do to be better as a boss and put it in my next book. Over the years the stories were all different but the problems with the bosses were much the same. I'd just put

a checkmark on the already-listed complaint. Below is a fulfillment of that promise. Here is their list.

### If you are a Promoter Boss . . .

Have integrity. Be professional. Do not take too many risks. Keep
the books legitimate; don't spend money you don't have or which
is not in the budget. Keep your word. Focus, pay attention to details. Be on time. Do not gossip or lie. Get organized, and do not
lose everything including files, keys, or important documents.
When you say you are going to follow up or do something, do
it. Stay on tasks that need to be accomplished; manage your time
effectively. For men, do not be inappropriate with female employees; and, for female Promoter Bosses, do not flirt.

Promoters' themes for improvements are about honesty, integrity, time management, and professionalism. Please note that
most of the above are about performing the TASK more effectively. Usually Promoters can slide by on their charm and relationship skills, but effective tasking seems to elude some. One
student quoted, "I like playing golf with him, and he's a fun guy.
But working for him is just too wild of a ride when I have a family to support."

### If you are a Planner Boss . . .

Be flexible, loosen up, try accepting and liking the human race.
People make mistakes, so be more forgiving and less strict. Get
out of your rut and try thinking out of the box. Methodical is
not a good management style; a little creativity and energy here,
please.

Manage your anger. Try trusting us not to screw up. Forget the past, manage for today; it's a new day and times have
changed. Please try to look on the bright side; maybe the glass
is really half full. Take a people skills course. Being kind is often
more important than being right. Make the punishment match
the crime. We know rules are rules, but sometimes it shows kindness of heart to bend them.

Planners' themes for improving are about building relation-ship, keeping relationships, and improving relationships. Com-pared to the Promoters and Peacekeepers, we find the Planners needing to improve upon totally opposite traits. Planners are logic based, practical, and task oriented. To be a good leader they must find their heart and throw some emotion into the mix. And some thought to speeding up processes in order to keep things moving might be important here also.

**If you are a Producer Boss . . .**

Don't manage through fear. Try loosening the grip on your con-trol lever. Showing you have a heart is not a bad thing. You are squeezing the life out of all of us. Your cunning promotes deceit. Rule of terror does not work. We understand you want it yester-day but a little compassion would go a long way. Your unfair ac-cusations pierce our souls. Don't be a workaholic or rage-aholic. It isn't always about you. Try not to make us feel hated. You use us for traction. Don't walk up our backs trying to get to the top. You are opportunistic and looking out for number one. Manip-ulation and dominance is paralyzing, not productive. Winning isn't everything or the only thing, it's people that count.

Producers' themes for improvement are like the Planners—relationships, kindness, and compassion.

If you are a Producer/ Planner combination or Planner/Pro-ducer you could be so logic based and task oriented that you don't understand people, or they frustrate you so much that trying to relate seems impossible. Here is a tip—make it a task to relate. Find out about your employees lives, hopes, and dreams. If you are a leader operating in more of your blind spots than strengths, I'm here to tell you, you are inflicting a great deal of misery on people and have probably lost some extremely gifted employees along the way. Please keep reading and try hard to apply these concepts to your work and personal life. Your relationships will improve and hopefully you will feel better about yourself.

**If you are a Peacekeeper Boss . . .**

Assert yourself. Make a decision. Stop being so overwhelmed—
we are here to help. Tell us what we need to know; we don't read
minds. Rome is burning and you are fiddling; show some sense
of urgency. Our team is rotting, molding, and growing stagnant;
lead, follow, or get out of the way. Take a stand; you can't please
all the people all the time. Fish or cut bait . . . do something. No
decision is not a decision . . . it is default! Don't withdraw into
silence, keep the dialogue going. Insisting you stay in your comfort zone is selfish. Show some spine. Man or woman up. Your
kindness is killing us; we need some leadership here, not a pal.
Quit hiding behind silence and unproductive procrastination.
Risk, take a chance, change, move forward.

Peacekeepers' themes for improvement are tasking, being assertive, and being decisive. Tasking is also the theme for Promoters; if you are a Peacekeeper with a backup score of Promoter or
a Promoter/Peacekeeper, get your act together; your people skills
are great but your lack of action style hurts your team. Make a
plan and work the plan. A job well begun is half done.

Please note that in the situations above, often the four personality types are operating in their blind spots or weaknesses and
not their strengths. To be a great leader you must be constantly
self-monitoring. In every situation ask yourself, "Where am I—
strength or blind spot?" Stick with your strengths and you and your
employees will profit. This chart was in the Family section and
the Marriage section, but it's vital in the Coworker section also.

CHAPTER 16

# ACTION PLAN FOR THE WORKPLACE

## KEY ACTION STRATEGIES FOR INDIVIDUAL EMPLOYEES

The saying, "You are only as strong as your weakest player," applies to work as well as sports. The key action strategies below focus first on the individual and second on leadership. When each player understands his or her self and others, it makes for stronger team members. A team of strong members is a winning team.

### Action Strategy #1

Understand your strengths and work on positioning yourself into areas that use your strengths. For example, if you are relationship oriented and in a tasking job, try to move to something that works more with relating, either with other staff members or the public. It will serve both you and the company better if you are using your natural gifts and talents in your job. The workplace is where you spend most of your waking hours . . . shouldn't that be where you use your natural gifts and talents?

## Action Strategy #2

Understanding the Silent Questions Team Members Ask (chart found later in this chapter) will help you be more effective with upper management and your peers. Make sure you know others' silent questions and act in a manner that reassures them that you have the answers to their questions.

## Action Strategy #3

Study the How to Relate to each Personality Type chart again in Chapter 14. Make sure you are speaking the personality language of your boss and coworkers as you communicate and work with them. You want to be heard, and knowing who they are will help you make the conversation connection. Present all written materials in a style that will best suit their type.

## Action Strategy #4

Read all the leadership tips. You might be the boss someday and you want to be an effective one.

## Action Strategy #5

This Personality Type Summary for the Coworkers and the Workplace is to encapsulate all the remaining information you should know about yourself and those you work with both in upper management and subordinates.

The chart on the next page will help you manage yourself and others, both upward and downward. In seeking a promotion or in a job search, be sure to communicate your attributes and key strengths throughout the process.

## PERSONALITY TYPE SUMMARY FOR COWORKERS AND THE WORKPLACE

| Workplace | Promoter | Planner | Producer | Peacekeeper |
|---|---|---|---|---|
| I tend to FOCUS on: | Possibilities, options/ people | Practical applications/quality | Possibilities, goals/ results | Practical solutions and people's needs/ feelings |
| ROLES I naturally play at work: | Motivator, energizer | Analyzer, record keeper | Leader, results person | Diplomat, solution seeker |
| Personally I NEED: | Affirmations, recognition, camaraderie | Affiliation, to contribute, order | Competency, respect, to win | Steady pace, independent, sense of worth |
| My style of COMMUNICATION is: | Direct—I tell vs. ask | Indirect—ask questions vs. make statements | Direct—I tell vs. ask | Indirect—ask questions vs. make statements |
| At work I PREFER: | The start, challenge, freedom, flexibility, doing things the *fun way* | The process, developing systems, accuracy, doing it the *right way* | The finish, winning, control, results, doing things *my way* | The interaction, relationships, stability, calm, doing things on *my time table* |

## Action Strategy #6 Understanding Conflict

All relationships have stressful and adverse conditions which can bring conflict. Conflict or adverse conditions tend to move us to our blind spots. The chart below, when read from left to right, tells what we think of each of the four personality types under adverse conditions. Even people with our own personality type can annoy us. The first entry on the chart is what a Promoter thinks of another Promoter when conflict is present. Then the next box is what a Promoter thinks of a Planner and so on reading across.

## TYPES UNDER ADVERSE CONDITIONS

| During Adversity | Promoter | Planner | Producer | Peacekeeper |
|---|---|---|---|---|
| Promoters view other types as: | Too talkative, superficial, ball dropper, untrustworthy | Nit picky, rigid, unfeeling, critical | No people skills, pushy, opinionated | Noncommittal, overwhelmed, too timid, indecisive |
| Planners view other types as: | Hyper, jokester, rule bender, exaggerator | Inflexible, too precise, too cautious, too detailed | Loose cannon, unrealistic, dangerous | Inconsistent, impractical, too emotional, dreamer |
| Producers view other types as: | Disingenuous, too familiar, inconsistent, irresponsible | Boring, not quick, stuck in a rut, negative | Aggressive, dogmatic, controlling, impulsive | Stubborn, passive, weak, lazy |
| Peacekeepers view other types as: | Inauthentic, no principles, fibber, immature | No finesse, outspoken, rude, opinionated | Insensitive, controlling, frightening, self-serving | Unreliable, unrealistic, too needy, nonresponsive |

If you are married, this chart could also apply to you and your spouse during conflict. Study the chart together and talk it out. Remember to listen more than you talk. Listen for feelings. What feeling is your partner or coworker trying to express? Don't shut the other person down with your desire to get your side of this story in at the moment. Once you really understand the other person's feelings, feedback what you think you heard. Ask him or her if you got it right. Hold back on having your say in this moment. If this can be just about the other person this time, then when it is your turn to express your feelings you will have modeled how to just listen and make it solely about the other person. Hopefully your partner or coworker will give you that same opportunity. This takes a lot of maturity and grace but it's doable and it works. Partners or coworkers who feel heard are not trying to fight to have their say; that's when they can become listeners.

As you finish reading this chart, ask yourself, "How can I profit from this information? Is that where I go when stressed? What can I change, what can I enrich?" Also ask yourself if you are in the right job. Are you able to use your natural strength more than less of the time? Job satisfaction scores are highest when the employees are working in their strengths. If you are giving off positive energy because you like your job and it's a good fit, then you are doing your part to add value to the group or team and probably reducing stress. There is a correlation between job satisfaction and team stress.

## Action Strategy #7 Understand Personality Types Conflict Styles

How do the four types handle conflict? Each situation on any given day will give you a plethora of answers. Keeping in mind the task and relationship orientation of the four types, you can make some assumptions that often hold true. Conflicts are relational or task, and sometimes a combination of both.

Relational conflict examples: daily annoyances, dirty motives, jealousy, grudges, gossip, backstabbing, petty grievances, perceived betrayals to employees. This list is about PEOPLE.

Task conflict examples: differences over procedures, processes, or outcomes. Awful unforeseen happenings, budget problems, accidents, unrealistic deadlines, incorrect assumptions, incorrect data, and curve balls are examples of task sources for conflict. This list is about PROBLEMS.

**Promoters** are relationship oriented and emotion based. With these two core traits they will try to protect relationships at all costs. They will come at the conflict from a relational problem-solving mode, trying to keep people, feelings, and emotions out of it as best they can. Whether it's a task conflict, a relational conflict, or a combination of both, most Promoters are not comfortable as conflict resolvers. They just want the problem to go away and everyone to get along. Of course, in a leadership role they must resolve conflict. They can do it but their big heart for the humanoids is going to hold them back from getting too tough. They will often err on addressing too easily both the task, and especially, the relationship side of the problem. It's their strong people skills that eventually get the conflict worked out. Often they are able to preserve the relationships while solving the problem.

**Planners** are task oriented and logic based. Quick to figure out if this is a task problem, a relationship problem, or some of both, they start to deal with each component of the problem. Planners are comfortable with a task problem, which they do not mind figuring out and nailing down ASAP. They can be equally hard on the people.

Sometimes they can be too heavy-handed where people are concerned. As my mother always says, "You get more flies with honey than vinegar." Some Planners should remember this wise advice when it comes to people. Sometimes Planners and everyone else involved would be better served with a little more relating and a little less tasking. However, Planners are good at solving the problem even if they sometimes leave a trail of hurt feelings and wounded egos.

**Producers** are task oriented and logic based. Conflict is stopping progress so let's deal with it and move forward. Very confident in conflicts, they quickly figure out who or what is wrong and make it right. Producers will be tough on both the problems and the people. Their no-nonsense approach cuts through the issues and personalities and gets to the bottom of what has to be fixed. The expression, "Who do we have to kill to get the job done?," can apply to an overzealous Producer who made it his or her mission to fix the problem and eliminate the conflict. They do not suffer foolish emotions. They might say put your personal feelings aside for the good of the project. Suck it up and move on. Fix it now! They are not worried about winning a popularity contest. They just want to fix it and head to the finish line in strength and competency.

**Peacekeepers** are relationship oriented and emotion based; conflict and confrontation eats their lunch. But they have a personality trait that is valuable to them and everyone else involved. They are natural-born diplomats. Of the four types, Peacekeepers have the best listening skills, can stay mutual and neutral with both sides and are very adept at seeking solutions that will satisfy most. They are going to walk softly and compassionately while negotiating conflict. Peacekeepers are going to go easier on the problem and the people. They might take longer but team relationships will be in better condition when the conflict is over if a Peacekeeper is in charge.

## KEY ACTION STRATEGIES FOR LEADERSHIP

Leaders, you have a great deal of power and influence. You affect more lives than just your own. For successful relationships with everyone you lead or report to, you need strong people skills. Knowing and using the Action Strategies below will add value to your leadership and people skills.

### Action Strategy #1

Maybe you are not the CEO of a Fortune 500 company but you are a leader in your community, church, a coach, or the leader of your family. Here are some things you need to know about people who are working for and with you. People want leadership, they want you to be the best you can be, and they want to know you have their best interests at heart. The chart on the next page shows the three silent questions that must be answered by a leader for his or her group to feel successful and probably be successful. All three are core components for good leadership but knowing the priority order for each personality type is key for any good leader. Knowing what your people are thinking helps you to respond with greater insight and meet their needs.

## SILENT QUESTIONS TEAM MEMBERS ASK

| | Promoter | Planner | Producer | Peacekeeper |
|---|---|---|---|---|
| Can I TRUST you?<br><br>Do you have INTEGRITY? | Trust is the **second** priority question this group needs to have answered. | Integrity and your word is your bond = **number one** for this group. | Trusting you to get it done and do it expediently is **second** for this group. | Trust is the **second** priority question this group needs answered. |
| Do you have the KNOWLEDGE?<br><br>Are you COMPETENT? | Knowing what you are doing is the **third** priority question this group wants to have answered. | With a past/history orientation the **second** priority this group wants to know is—have you done your homework? | Being competent is core to this group; a big **number one**. | Knowing what you are doing is the **third** priority question this group wants answered. |
| Do you CARE about me?<br><br>Do you UNDERSTAND? me? | Heart-filled, emotions based and relationship oriented; these are their **number one** priority questions. | Logic based and task oriented; these relationship questions rank **third** for this group. | Logic based and task oriented; these relationship questions rank **last** for this group. | Heart-filled emotion based and relationship oriented; these are their **number one** priority questions. |

Note that Promoters and Peacekeepers have the relationship questions as their number one; Planners and Producers place them last in their order on these three sets of questions. Trust is core in any relationship.

## Action Strategy #2

Now that you know the different personality types and the task and relationship components, try to put the right people in the jobs that best fit their personality type. People do better when they have a natural gift and desire for what they are doing.

## Action Strategy #3

Review the Personality Type Leadership Traits and try to practice a strength and eliminate a weakness today. Also read again the Toxic Boss list to make sure you aren't reflecting any of these traits. You get extra points if you don't skip the tips for employees below. Good leaders need to know what their people think. Flip back to the Marriage section and look over the two triangles for marital foundations. Make sure you are not creating a fear-based environment for your employees or team members. If you skipped the three charts in Chapter 3, go back and read them. They will give you more insight into yourself and the people who work for or with you. The previous charts will help you manage yourself and others, both upward and downward. In seeking a promotion or in a job search, be sure to get all your attributes above into your resume or story.

## Action Strategy #4

Read the whole Coworker section. If you saw the Leadership chapter and skipped right to it, your employee who is reading this now knows way more about how to manage people than you do.

## Action Strategy #5

Review all seven Key Action Strategies for Individual Employees in the beginning of the chapter. As a leader you need to know what your people know and are thinking. Pay close attention to the Conflict Resolution information; this could save you from headaches and heartburn.

## KEY ACTION STRATEGIES FOR THE JOB SEARCH

One of my Certified People Skills Trainers is a career coach who has been coaching people back to work for over fifteen years, in good markets and bad. She coaches her clients differently for each type of market. When she coaches clients in good "bull" markets in which the unemployment rate is low, she spends a good deal of time coaching them to find careers that match their personality types. She has them review their strengths, preferences, and blind spots carefully, then look for work that calls for what comes naturally to them.

For instance, Promoters tend to do well in sales, sales support or motivational type positions. If you are a Promoter/Producer, you can excel at both motivating people to buy and closing deals! You can tell interviewers that you are great at building and leading teams, as well as motivating participation of community leaders, volunteers and staff. In the non-profit world, you might consider positions in fund development or in positions building corporate partnerships. If you are a Planner, you would enjoy jobs that require systematic, analytical thinking, detail, and a measure of perfectionism. Accounting, technology, systems analysis, quality assurance, regulatory compliance and data management are right up your alley. Producers do well managing—projects, staff, tasks, departments, programs—anything that takes skill for getting the job done on time and under budget. And you Peacekeepers are vital in every organization for gaining consensus among team members as well as with customers. You make good counselors, mediators, negotiators, team builders and advisors. Shop for a job fit that matches your personality type and you'll be one who says, "I love my job!"

And once you get that dream job, be sure to take your new understanding to work with you! Don't be like the Planner / Producer who worked in a medical billing office with a department manager who was a Promoter. (How she ended up managing that department is beyond me!) Ms. Planner / Producer grumbled with resentment when she was terminated from that job "for no good reason." According to her, she was the only one who met their Friday deadlines and got to go home on time while everyone else always had to stay late to get the billing done. But what was the real story? It seems that every Friday Ms. Promoter-Manager invited the entire team to lunch. Everyone went except—you got it—our friend, Ms. Planner / Producer, who stayed behind to finish the work and end the day with a haughty "I told you not to go" over her shoulder to the rest of the team as they stayed late. She still might have that job today if she had only recognized that she needed to put on a Promoter T-shirt over that royal blue Planner shirt every once in a while and build relationship! She was so bent on the task; she forgot she was part of a team. Finding the right job is one thing, keeping it takes the same attention to how you fit into the team around you.

But what about times when the job market tanks and the unemployment rate soars? What do you do if you are one of those whose company has either "restructured" you out of a job or simply gone out of business and left you and your colleagues applying for unemployment? While we can focus on finding the best career fit for our personality types in good markets, many people find themselves focusing on simply finding any J-O-B that will pay the rent or mortgage now and keep them above water.

If you haven't searched for work in some years, you have no doubt found that the job search has changed drastically. Unemployed career veterans, comfortable in their jobs for years, now face an employer's ("buyer's") market and a job search that is largely conducted in cyberspace. It even seems to some as though "human" has been taken out of Human Resources when it comes to the search. Now you're going to have to learn to put your skills and experience on a resume that will make it through the maze of Application Tracking Software (ATS) before a human even sees it! Competition can be brutal and age discrimination is real at both ends of the age continuum. It will be important for you to understand how you deal with change so that you won't slide into despair. Here are some strategies for keeping yourself motivated to find work.

### Action Strategy #1: KNOW THYSELF!

Look back at the charts to see how your personality type will tend to react to, and deal with, change. Peacekeepers may face it with a sense of dread, go to bed and pull the covers up over their heads because dealing with change is just too overwhelming. Planners could feel an initial sense of betrayal and rush to put their own method into place for the search. Producers usually go for an immediate "fix," what my friend calls a "knee-jerk" decision to take "any" job and end up underemployed with no opportunity to continue to search or interview. Take a deep breath, Producers. Whatever your type, job loss means huge change. And huge change means you will have to look at the blind spots in your type and find ways to overcome them.

### Action Strategy #2: BE TEACHABLE!

One of the greatest challenges my Career Coach friend faces in dealing with her clients is convincing them that if they want a job, they will have to accept today's new search methods. What? More change?! Isn't job loss bad enough? Sorry, the job search has changed.

Her greatest challenge is with Producers whose need to "do it my way" (which, by the way, may actually have worked for Producer-Managers for many years), only serves to delay a positive outcome. Second on her "challenge" list are the Promoters who sit through her workshops and coaching sessions, neglecting to take note—or notes!—and just figure they'll get through the search as they always have, charming some future employer into an offer. She can almost hear them thinking as she teaches: "Blah, blah, blah . . . yeah, yeah, yeah." Unfortunately, new selective software doesn't recognize charm and, though it frustrates Promoters to deal with the seemingly tedious task of learning keyword and formatting rules, if you want an invitation to HR, you will have to suck it up and learn to use the new system. You Planners will be initially skeptical of systems you haven't devised yourself, but you'll eventually grab the new rules like a secure lifeline because rules have always worked for you. And through it all, you Peacekeepers will sit looking like deer in the headlights wondering what happened to your world and how you are ever going to learn so much detail. Do not go back to bed, Peacekeepers! You can do this. In fact, you all can do this.

But wait, there's more, just a little more with which to deal. If this new search system isn't enough of a challenge to your "being teachable," you may just find yourself being interviewed by a decision maker-manager who is decades younger than you! Young managers, asked to list their greatest concerns for veteran workers, usually place "rigid and un-teachable" among their top five. So, here's another exciting opportunity for you to learn how to present yourself to today's young managers. I want to generalize just a few pointers good for all personality types facing a challenging age gap. Are you ready to be teachable? Take a deep breath, here we go:

- DON'T act like a parent; don't say, "I have a son, daughter or grandchild your age!" This is condescending. No manager wants to be treated like a child.

- Don't make even slightly negative comments about technology. This isn't the "good old days." One of young management's greatest concerns about older workers is their lack of technical skills.

- Learn the language of the workplace. In today's general market, that means learning Microsoft Office Suite. Find an adult community class and start learning! Then you can proudly say you are a "lifelong learner."

- LEARN whatever new skill your industry requires; stay productive! Tell the interviewer you are highly productive; you've used this search time to acquire or upgrade your skills.

There are many other practical strategies for overcoming age-ism, whatever your personality type, all of which you can learn online or in job search workshops, but the above pointers deal with being teachable. Recognize your personality type's points of resistance or fear. Be honest if your skill levels need updating. Whatever your personality type, LEARN what you need to know and practice to find work!

**Action Strategy #3: BE REALISTIC!**

When times are tough, we can't always have the job that fits our type the best. But we're grown-ups, right? We didn't always get what we wanted in life and that goes for jobs, too, sometimes. When the job market is tough, we might have to put on one of our back-up personality type shirts to get the job and then do it well.

One of my friend's clients had been a very successful finance manager in a car dealership but when the recession hit, he found himself at first jobless, then without savings, and eventually homeless with a wife and two children in an agency's housing program. He wanted work, yes, but something new. Something that wouldn't require the same long tedious hours. He was a Promoter and wanted something flexible and fun. For weeks he looked for other opportunities but couldn't find anything. He dreaded going back to the auto dealerships where he'd end up in finance again. Then one week he showed up for his coaching session with an upbeat attitude and a new readiness to go back to what he'd always done. "What happened?" my friend asked. "Well, it was something you said in the last workshop. You said, 'Sometimes the job is tough, it's not want we want to do. That's why we call it work and not fun.'" He ended up back in the auto industry, working hard long hours again but doing very well and feeling very productive.

In tough markets we sometimes have to wear the strengths of our back up types that don't fit just right. But what we can do is find something to do outside of work that fulfills our need to function within our main strengths. So, find a place to volunteer! Donate your creativity, management skills, counseling, or financial skills to a worthy organization that will be grateful for your help!

## THE COWORKER SUMMARY

To apply or not to apply this knowledge, that is the question. What are you going to do with the information in this section now that you have read it? If you are married and skipped the Marriage section, I encourage you to go back and read that. Take to heart all the information in that section. Why? If you and your spouse/mate talk about this and work on it together, you will have had some out-of-office experience and probably another personality type to practice and learn from. This will be a mutual and shared experience on the home front. At work, unless you can talk a coworker into reading the book or ask management to contact my company for certification or training, you may have to apply these principles alone. But if you understand and self-manage better than ever before, you will see change in yourself and the way you respond. When you talk to fellow employees in their personality language, even if they don't know their own language, you will see a difference. This might not be instant gratification, but your new awareness, desire, and stronger people skills will pay off. Change can only begin with you. Remember, managing the differences makes all the difference.

My contact information is at the end of the book. I would treasure hearing the story of your journey to understanding personality types in your workplace.

*A Friend is a place we can find*
*where we run when life's less than kind.*
*There we laugh and we cry*
*and see love in dear eyes,*
*then depart with the weight left behind.*

# SECTION V

# FRIENDS

*Friends, Freedom, and Fun*

As you begin this last section of the book, you know your personality type. Each personality type brings core strengths and blind spots to family, work, and friends. In this section we explore friendship and what we bring to a friendship. Friendships are supposed to be the frosting on the relational cake. Knowing more about yourself and the personality type of each friend will help you manage and relate better for more rewarding friendships.

For Promoters, making and having friends is a specialty. You like people and people like you. You are warm, charming, charismatic, and fun. What's not to like? People magnets of the highest order, you make friends in restaurant bathrooms and on airplanes. You probably have a large circle of friends, some more intimate than others. Popularity is important to you so this section on Friends will help you have an improved strategy for adding to the quality of the friendships you currently have as well as new ones.

Planners, I'm going to be right up front with you. I have no controlled studies, empirical data, or scientifically conducted interviews. But I've listened to thousands of people, as have my certified trainers, and we have all kept notes. It's not controlled but it's the facts as the personality types told them to us. We have years and years of observation, unlimited time logged with people on teams during and after work, listening to them and making copious notes. We have a plentitude of hours from retreat weekends where people shared their thoughts and hearts with us. We listened and later recorded what we heard from Planners about friendship. Plus, you will be happy to know three of my most senior certified trainers are blue Planners. We understand your loyalty, being there when needed, and going the extra mile in thoughtfulness. True blue friends you are.

Producers, I do not have any bottom line exact science methods for the making or maintenance of highly effective friendships. No validated competency studies or best practices. Friendship is relationship first and of course tasking plays a big role if you are going on an adventure or trying to accomplish some project together. Loyalty, trust, and mutual respect are hard to measure and quantify. Two of my red Producer certified trainers and I have given careful thought to your needs in this section. You are the friend who thinks up what to do and gets it done. Not usually content just to hang out, you will organize an outing, a helpful community project, or a game of some kind at the very least. You are the action-oriented friend and usually the leader of the pack. Everyone knows there will be something going on when you are around. You are not into dull moments or contemplating your navel.

Thank you, Peacekeepers. You will read this and not worry if it is documented or scientific. You will read it with your heart and decide if it agrees with your truth about friendship or not. I hope it does because you are some of the most accepting friends on the planet. You get people. Combined with your compassion, that is an awesome combination. Giving grace and acceptance is your specialty. You make people feel special and cared about. You are the kindest friend of all the personality types.

# CHAPTER 17

# A FRIEND IS . . .

B elow is a collaborative definition of Friendship. All four personality types had input into this definition.

Freedom is the environment in which true friendship lives.
Friendship requires no contract, license, or certificate—no paper-
work or Social Security number necessary. Unlike your relatives,
you were able to choose these people yourself. You volunteered
for friendship.

Friendship is easier to enter and exit than any other meaning-
ful relationship. This relationship comes with less responsibility
than being a spouse, parent, or an employee. There are fewer
opportunities for relationship fatigue because you usually do not
live with each other. The weight of obligations is removed because you are not required to feed, clothe, or shelter your friends
on a regular basis.

Being with a friend is less work and frequently more fun than
family or people at your job. Trust, candor, honesty, and reci-
procity can thrive in friendship. The voluntary nature of this
interdependent relationship is less structured, with fewer social
norms and societal expectations, thus, more freedom. Friendship
is a distinctive kind of concern for another person.

Because of the element of freedom, it is a different kind of
love, which builds an immense faith in each other and the potential for great joy. These levels of faith, trust, respect, acceptance

of individuality, vulnerability, compassion, and empathy are qualities we sometimes experience only with friends. The benefits of a close mutual friendship are immense, to understanding and being understood. For many of us, our greatest desire is to know and be known in an environment of safety. Remember the lyrics of the theme song of the popular television sitcom *Cheers* that describes a place where "everybody knows your name" and you are always welcome.

We all deeply need love, acceptance, and forgiveness and, sadly, often do not find these needs met in our primary relationships. We, therefore, look to friends to have our needs met. Loyalty, having each others' best interests at heart, having a determined advocate in your corner, unconditional acceptance and love can often be found in its purest form in friendships. The opportunity to share from the core of your being and return the gift of listening is the harmony of friendship. A quote from Dorothy Parker sums it up, "Constant use had not worn ragged the fabric of their friendship."

My experience with friendship has taught me that it truly is my most freeing relationship. Soul sharing, authenticity, equality, emotional release, purity of spirit, and more consistent opportunities for unencumbered joy are the hallmarks of my friendships. True friendship is a blessed gift to all humans.

Being a Promoter I love people. I am blessed to have lots of friends. Promoters can handle multiple friendships because they like variety and can multitask.

We have an on-the-go spirit about us, which works for a come-one, come-all philosophy. Life's a party; everyone is invited. But friendship has degrees of intimacy. Not every friendship is a deep sharing soul mate relationship.

Soul mate friends cannot save you from the depth of a season of emotional despair, a life-threatening illness or the loss of a loved one, but they can make the way more bearable. Just the act of being there, listening, loving, and even serving one day at a time is the core of soul friends. My circle of soul mates never falters, never leaves even when I know I've drained them. They never quit being there for me. Sometimes they have been there to just remind me to breathe because fear of the future was choking me. They have shined their hope for me into my life when it has seemed dark and hopeless. They carried me in prayer when I could barely look up and mutter, "Help."

Soul friends endure all seasons, and when the sunshine times in life are bright they are there to celebrate. From sharing good news phone calls to girls' getaways, my soul friends are true, loyal, and a whole lot of fun to travel with on this journey called life. My soul friends always bring the joy. I thank and love you, soul mate friends.

A favorite author of mine, Henry Nouwen, articulates soul mate friends this way: "When we honestly ask ourselves which person in our life means the most to us, we often find that it is those who, instead of giving advice, solutions, or cures, have chosen rather to share our pain and touch our wounds with a warm and tender hand. The friend who can be silent with us in a moment of despair or confusion, who can stay with us in an hour of grief and bereavement, who can tolerate not knowing, not curing, not healing, and face with us the reality of our powerlessness, that is a friend who cares."

The deep soulful friendship that has been described above is a continual ebb and flow of a constant friendship that is at the heart of the core of your life. But friendship has degrees. Terms like "Circle of Friends," or "Friendship Ladder," and "Primary and Secondary Friends," help you define the degrees. Whether it's a symbolic "Friend Ladder," with you and your dearest friend sitting on the top rung, or a group of three or four friends that join hands in a figurative circle, a friend or friends are vital to good mental health, a song in your heart, and a smile on your face.

Friends for a season or friends for a reason are part of our history. Neighbors become close friends for as long as you live in the neighborhood. Maybe it continues, maybe not. We have lived in the same neighborhood for thirty-eight years. First I met another mother at the playground. We had kids the same age. Then a woman with two boys about my boys' ages moved in a few doors down. She introduced me to her friend four streets over, who brought two girlfriends and a bachelor, so the group began. The husbands met and we all played volleyball and barbequed at one of our homes every weekend. Over the years, we have shared joys and sorrows. Been there for each other in the ups and downs of life.

Another place we meet friends for a reason is as parents. While sitting in the bleachers and cheering on our children, we often make friends with other parents. This cheering together can be for a season or a lifetime.

Friends from book clubs or Bible studies are drawn together around a common interest. Work friends, organization friends like fellow Friends of the Library or gardening club, golfing buddies, or your card group all add to the texture and soul of our lives. Some stay till death do us part and others drift away. Some season or reason friends we bare our soul to, and others we just enjoy our time spent together. The degree of intimacy varies as much as the personality types of the friends.

For many of us, we still are close with high school and college friends. I know someone who meets every year with three other friends from grade school, which really defines "old friends." She is a Planner and the shepherd of the group.

Planners are usually very good at maintaining long-term relationships. If you look closely at your class reunion committee, it's the Planners and the Producers who are chairing the event and making it happen. The Planners have kept addresses and contact information over the years. The Producers are getting the place and hiring the caterers. The Promoters and the Peacekeepers are adding the relational touches and planning the social mixers.

My husband Fred and I are still in close relationships with college and early married couples friends. We don't live in the same areas with our college friends, but on those quarterly times me meet, we pick right up where we let off. Friends from early in our marriage are often part of our holiday celebrations. Friendships that have the qualities to last a lifetime are pure gold.

Over the years I've heard many stories of fellow travelers who weather a transatlantic flight or an around the world cruise who became "new best friends" for the duration of the trip. Sometimes our hearts connect momentarily with a total stranger for such a time as this. Other times the relationship continues.

We first met a couple at a dude ranch in Montana thirty years ago, who became dear friends. Spending time together for one week convinced us we needed to be intentional about this new friendship. We booked the same week for the following year and then year after year. With grown children, we don't go to the dude ranch anymore, but we see those friends every chance we get, even though we live miles apart. These fellow travelers have become like family.

We travel by recreational vehicle these days. Both my husband and I have occupied enough airplane seats to last a lifetime. We are seeing America the beautiful on the highways and byways. Wonderful friendships started around our shared interest . . . RVing. Talk about becoming friends overnight. RVers are the friendliest people on earth—willing to guide you into a narrow parking site or help with a broken part. We have made wonderful new friends and strengthened old relationships through traveling together. Our friends from R-Gang, Monaco, Triple C, and other groups make traveling great fun.

Friendship can mean a lifetime best friend or a stranger on a train who you meet, befriend, and part with, both richer for your time together.

# CHAPTER 18

# ENRICHING
# FRIENDSHIPS

The next chart is the compilation of my certified trainers' and my records of the results of numerous training sessions and retreats. We asked the participants to list the good things and the not-so-good things about being in a friendship with them. Please notice that there is an "Areas to Work on" right below the list of "Good Things." Our strengths taken too far can be not so good! Please read the Male and Female parts. There is something to learn about yourself and your friends that will enrich your relationships.

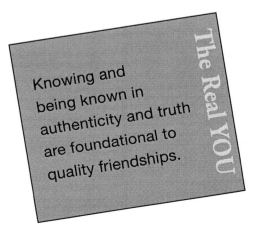

Knowing and being known in authenticity and truth are foundational to quality friendships.

The Real YOU

# PROMOTER MALE

### Good Things

- We know we have more heart and relationships skills than some of our male counterparts. We truly care about people. We make friends easily.
- We are naturally good at making things fun and eventful. From volunteer work projects to sports, we bring the fun. We know we are fun; others know we are fun. It's a core part of who we are.
- We are pretty good listeners for guys. But we are better at cheering you up than trying to solve your problems. Cheering up is more fun.
- We do not take friendship lightly. We know the value a friend's love brings to us and us to them.
- We believe the more the merrier.
- We are highly verbal and good at honest affirmations. We also love you enough to do "Tough Love" when necessary.
- No matter how miserable a situation, we can always find a bright side. And we encourage you with it.
- We attract excitement.

### Areas to Work on

- Don't give us the original of anything. We don't want that much responsibility.
- We run late because we have too many irons in the fire and believe we can quickly do one more thing. Like to cram a lot into life. Don't want any dull moments.
- We have been known to create chaos to prevent boredom.
- Close enough is good enough. We know it drives the Planners crazy.
- People naturally follow us . . . the problem is we often don't know where we are going.
- We can be impulsive.
- We like to tell our stories. Because things happen to us that don't happen to other guys. If it's going to be unconventional, it's going to happen to us. We are magnets for the can you believe this unbelievable thing that happened to me?
- Murphy's Law and Ripley's Believe It or Not seem to find us.

# PROMOTER FEMALE

## Good Things

- We are empathetic, not sympathetic.
- You can call us at 4:00 in the morning. We are spontaneous.
- We are always going to try to find some sun in your cloudy day. We are the eternal optimists.
- Always up for a little retail shopping therapy.
- We have good instincts. Between our heart and our gut hunches we give pretty good advice. It comes from a deep heart of caring.
- We are natural-born shrinks. Just a little detail like the formal education is missing.
- We are cheerleaders for your life. We are fun to be with. We can turn a boring anything into a circus you will want to tell your other friends about.
- We are a lot of love and just a little crazy.
- People magnets. We make friends in restaurant bathrooms. If anyone is going to talk in an elevator, it's a Promoter.
- We see life as an exciting adventure and we want everyone to participate.
- Spontaneity keeps our friendships energized and fresh.
- Our close-enough attitudes keep us on the move, taking our friends along for a joy-filled unpredictable ride.

## Areas to Work on

- Have us bring the dessert not the appetizers; we are often late.
- We are trying not to share that we know how you feel, with our own story. We know we should just listen to yours in your moment of need. Our hearts want to be there for you but our mouths get in the way. We know we are talkers.
- We are guilty of interjecting with sound bite comments. Our energy and enthusiasm get the best of us, and we interrupt.
- Have 365 best friends—one for every day of the year. We also exaggerate. Bigger is better.
- We like to be noticed. From clothes to accessories to furnishings, we know we can go way out of the box. "Did anyone say bling?"
- Life for us is a miniseries and we love the high drama in our starring role. We really do want you for a friend and not just an audience.
- To be a better friend we need to remember this social interacting policy, "So there you are . . . here I am." But we rush in with our latest wild story and take center stage. Eventually we get around to others, because we do care.
- "If it feels good, do a bunch of it." "If one looks cute on you, get another one in a different color."
- Planning isn't our strength. Forgetful . . . call or text us the morning of the event.

# PLANNER MALE

| Good Things |
| --- |
| • We are dependable; you can count on us. Our word is our bond. |
| • Very service oriented, ready to pitch in and do our part. We also have the tools for most jobs, kept in an organized manner. |
| • We like traditions and will be the one to maintain them. The guys' annual hunting, fishing, camping, golfing, hiking, or whatever trip tends to be kept alive by us. |
| • We are joiners. Good causes that preserve things and help the needy particularly appeal to us. |
| • We are logical and cautious. We look out for you. |
| • We are analytical so we are going to come up with lots of points of view to a situation. If you ask we will give you our honest opinion. |
| • Understand quality in things and friendships. |

| Areas to Work on |
| --- |
| • Frustrated with tardiness, disorganization, and flaky people. |
| • Don't like things to get messed up. We probably won't say anything, but we are coming right behind you cleaning and organizing. |
| • Can be neat-freaks. |
| • Overdo on the preparation of an event, then are critical of others who we think didn't do their part. |
| • Can over-commit, then get tired and grouchy. |
| • We are more workhorse than sprinter so sometimes you might think we are plodding along. |
| • Intimacy is hard for us because it is so unpredictable. |
| • Can be picky about things and people. |

# PLANNER FEMALE

## Good Things

- Our list will probably be the shortest. We are no nonsense and won't belabor a point.
- We are dependably there for you.
- Service is the name of our game. Driving to doctors, taking you to drop off your car, meals when you are sick, and doing thoughtful things without being asked.
- Consistency—we are along for the ride. Smooth or bumpy, we are with you.
- Loyal—we know how to stay in long-term friendships. Good at setting boundaries, we love you but are not pushovers.
- Really are "true blue" friends.
- Responsible—if something needs to be done, we will do it. We believe we organize more events than any other personality type. Bridal to baby showers, we are the hostesses.
- Quality is one of our hallmarks. We do things in a quality way. We go the extra mile.
- We like things of quality. We would rather have a small perfect diamond than a large one that's slightly flawed. Our gifts may be small but quality.
- We are generous with our belongings.
- You can borrow from us we have back stock on everything. From soup to soap we have spares in organized cupboards.
- Come to our house in case of a natural disaster. We are always prepared.
- We listen, take in your situation, and care.
- Yes, we clip coupons, but will share with you!

## Areas to Work on

- Being task oriented and logic based we struggle with intimacy sometimes. It takes us a while to trust. Letting people in is not always easy.
- Sharing from our heart can be hard. We play our emotional life close to the vest.
- We live a scheduled orderly life so sometimes we seem inflexible.
- We may be critical of how you are handling something, but we are still there for you.
- Sometimes our boundaries keep us from giving enough TLC.
- We like things done right. Can be perfectionists.
- Particular about our possessions, we need things to be well made.
- Consumer's guide is never far away. Research every purchase.
- When you borrow please return it exactly as we gave it to you.
- We've been accused of raining on parades. We can be brutally honest!
- We are accused of seeing the glass as half empty.
- We hate being wrong so we tend to place blame upon others.

## PRODUCER MALE

| Good Things |
| --- |
| • We are good at problem solving. |
| • We are good in a crisis, comfortable delegating and making quick decisions. |
| • We will take the leadership role. |
| • You can count on us to show up and do our part. |
| • We always have a plan for action or adventure. |
| • We are reliable, just a text or call away. Usually we'll get there. |
| • We go for it. Promoting making the relationship happen. |
| • We network and connect friend with other friends. |
| • Keep the group of friends alive and interacting. |

| Areas to Work on |
| --- |
| • We would rather take action than just listen. |
| • We are not always patient with other's way of doing things. |
| • We can be pushy and assertive. |
| • Compassion is sometimes hard for us. |
| • Keeping busy avoids intimacy, which can be hard for us. |
| • Can be opportunistic and jeopardize the friendship. |
| • We are conflicted between being the reliable friend and our job. Often workaholics, the job can come first. |

# PRODUCER FEMALE

| Good Things |
| --- |
| • We are good at initiating events, outings and parties. |
| • We make things happen. |
| • We are decisive and honest. |
| • We are adventuresome and daring. Be prepared to add new things to your life. |
| • Often, we'd rather have an adventure than lay by the pool. |
| • We are good at networking—helping your friends meet our friends, making just one big happy family. |
| • We are loyal. We will fight for you. |
| • Your best interests are often at the core of our actions. |

| Areas to Work on |
| --- |
| • Forceful make it happen style can be seen as bossy and controlling. |
| • If you ask for our opinion, we will give it good or bad. We might even give it without you asking. |
| • We'd rather solve your problem. Better at doing than being. |
| • We are loyal, but intimacy is sometimes difficult. Trust is a huge factor. |
| • We are afraid of being betrayed so we don't give our hearts away easily. |
| • Our strong desire to accomplish can make us seem hard and uncaring. |
| • Our demand for competency in others limits who we will engage in friendships with. We do not suffer foolish people. |
| • We can write off friendship with a hand gesture; try to pull us back in, we need it. |

## PEACEKEEPER MALE

| Good Things |
| --- |
| • We understand a person, which helps us to be a true friend. |
| • We are comfortable with emotions. |
| • We really care about our friends at the heart level. |
| • We really listen to you to hear the emotions under the story. |
| • We don't try to solve your problem, just let you know we hear you and are here. |
| • Patient and tolerant. |
| • Kindness is important to us. |

| Areas to Work on |
| --- |
| • Staying flexible is key to us. We care but a firm commitment is hard for us. |
| • We are easily overwhelmed with life's hectic pace. |
| • We have trouble combining our deep level of caring with an action commitment. |
| • We have the answers you need, but remember to ask for them, we won't volunteer. |
| • If you push us too far, we will be finished with our friendship. |

## PEACEKEEPER FEMALE

| Good Things |
| --- |
| • Friendships are one of our highest values. |
| • Heart to heart talks are our specialty. |
| • We are deeply compassionate. We get your joy or pain. |
| • We will be vulnerable to make you feel like you are not alone. |
| • Because of we make decisions with our heart, we give wise counsel. |
| • We are beside you emotionally and physically when possible. |
| • Caring and trust are hallmarks of our friendship. |

| Areas to Work on |
| --- |
| • We are non-confrontational so we often don't speak up. |
| • We like to be pursued, so you will probably need to call us. Besides we don't want to bother you. |
| • Our tender hearts just break for you and we cannot separate ourselves from your problems. |
| • Sometimes our indecisiveness and lack of organization makes us unable to physically be there for you. |
| • Often we just don't have our act together. So we let you down. |
| • If trust is broken we will not confront but go away quietly. |

# CHAPTER 19

# ACTION STEPS FOR A GOOD TIME

Friendship should be the fun, good times, and carefree adventures that other relationships sometimes don't offer. Another element of friendship is having someone there while you hear yourself talk—that wonderful listening ear that cares, doesn't judge, and is rooting for you to work out whatever is bothering you and move forward. From debriefing your day to describing a crisis, to have a trusted friend there for you is the ultimate joy in life. Friendship is one of life's treasures, and you need a plan to preserve that treasure.

## KEY ACTION STEPS FOR ENRICHING FRIENDSHIPS

**#1 Reread the definition of friendship.** Make a list of what you need from a friend and make a list of what you think you bring to your most important friendships. Also list what you could improve upon.

**#2 Explore the personality type of the friend or friends with which you would like to have a stronger relationship.** Then study the Friendship charts in this section. List five things you can do to customize and enrich your relationship with that friend.

**#3 Be intentional.** We give what we want to receive. Knowing what your friends give in a friendship, like listening or compassion or doing nice things for you, will also tell you what your friends want from friendship with you. We give out in relationship characteristics that which we would like in return.

If you have a **Promoter** friend or friends, remember they are encouragers who are good at affirming and they would like encouragement and affirmation returned. Tell them how much you value who they are and what their friendship means to you. A long laundry list of their attributes and qualities would be just fine with them. Maybe on a big poster . . . (kidding). Talk is not cheap to a Promoter! If you can say it in front of a large group—more's the better!

For **Planner** friends, loyalty, service, and trust are their core. To improve your friendship with Planners make sure you give these attributes back to them. Doing thoughtful things is paramount to Planners. Give acts of service back to them. They are sincere. A written note about the value of their friendship, without mistakes, on quality notepaper would mean a great deal to your Planner friends. Planners are card senders. Hallmark should love this group. They send cards for every occasion. Watch . . . they will send cards to you. Send cards also.

For **Producer** friends, remember they value achievement and accomplishment. Respect for a Red Producer is very key. So tell them what they've done and are to you that evokes your respect. If you commit to any of their projects, make sure you show up and do your part. Support them in their need to accomplish. Remember, just because they always make it happen and get it done does not mean they can't use a little TLC just like the rest of us.

For **Peacekeeper** friends, the kindest among us, be intentional about showing them acts of kindness. Peacekeeper friends value tolerance and compassion. Respect their need to defend the underdog and lend a helping hand.

They are crusaders for the marginalized and downtrodden. You don't have to march in their parades, but understand their strong need to do so and support them verbally. Peacekeepers know how to touch hearts and understand intimacy. Make sure you speak your heart with your Peacekeeper friends. Let them know how deeply you care.

Study the information for each personality type in this section. Knowing what your friends give to you in the friendship will also tell you what they would like to receive back from you. By paying attention to the way your friends treat you, you can learn how to be a better friend to them.

**#4 Know that the key success factors in friendships are the same as with every other group.** Here are the basics: understanding, trying to speak another's personality language, knowing what others value, and respond in kind. Add gentleness, faithfulness, kindness, grace, and patience, and you've got the formula for a successful friendship or any relationship.

# CONCLUSION

As this book concludes, favorite expressions, sayings, and bumper stickers from each personality type offer some insights and perspective into what each type might think about life and how they each approach relationships.

## YELLOW PROMOTER WILL TELL US . . .

- Live! Laugh! Love!

- You can't take it with you.

- Don't take yourself so seriously.

- Lighten up.

- Go with the flow.

- Close enough is good enough.

- Housework done properly can kill you.

- Throw it on the wall and see if it sticks.

- *Mas o menos.*

- I told you 50,000 times, stop exaggerating.

- Seize the day—*Carpe Diem.*

- I came, I saw, I did a little shopping.

- Live for the moment.
- Don't follow me, I'm lost.
- I used to have a handle on life but now it is broken.
- Create positive memories.
- Leap and the net will appear.
- It isn't if you win or lose; it's how you play the game.
- There are no winners or losers, only players.
- Play for fun.
- Gone crazy, be back soon.

## BLUE PLANNERS WILL TELL US . . .

- Your word is your bond.
- Keep calm, carry on.
- A place for everything and everything in its place.
- Get your act together.
- Do it right the first time.
- Cleanliness is next to godliness.
- Plan ahead.
- Be prepared.
- Get real—be serious.
- This is no laughing matter.
- Those of you who think you know everything really annoy those of us who do.
- Get your head out of the clouds.
- A stitch in time saves nine.

- I can be spontaneous if you'll give me enough time.

- According to my calculation, the problem doesn't even exist.

- If you think nobody cares about you, try missing a couple of payments.

- If money could talk, it would say goodbye.

- Make a plan and work the plan.

- Play by the rules.

## RED PRODUCERS WILL TELL US . . .

- A job well begun is half done.

- Lead, follow, or get out of the way.

- Time is money.

- Be ALERT. We need more Lerts!

- Do it right the first time!

- Knowledge is power.

- Proper preparation prevents poor performance.

- My way or the highway!

- I want it done yesterday.

- If you can't take the heat, get out of the kitchen.

- Get to the bottom line.

- Get real.

- Denial is NOT a river in Egypt.

- Who do we have to kill to get the job done?

- Make it Happen.

- He who dies with the most toys wins.

- He who hesitates is not only lost, but miles from the next exit.

- He who laughs last thinks slowest.

- Forget about world peace . . . visualize using your turn signal.

- Don't get even . . . get ahead.

- Show me a good loser and I'll show you a loser.

- You know there can only be one winner, did you still want to play?

- Play to win.

## GREEN PEACEKEEPERS WILL TELL US . . .

- Remember the Golden Rule.

- Peace at any price.

- Don't make waves.

- Stay cool, calm, and collected.

- No decision is a decision.

- Don't try to fence me in.

- Independence is a state of mind and a town.

- Think good thoughts.

- Bark less, wag more.

- People should live life in no particular way but their own.

- I used to be apathetic, now I just don't care.

- Hypochondria is one disease I have not gotten yet.

- The worst day of fishing is better than the best day at work.

- If I quit voting, will they all go away?

- Just because I'm wandering doesn't mean I'm lost.

- Experience is something you don't get until you need it.

- I haven't lost my mind; it's backed up on a cloud somewhere.

- I intend to live forever, so far so good.

- If at first you don't succeed, then try, try again.

- If at first you don't succeed, then skydiving is definitely not for you.

- I feel like I'm diagonally parked in a parallel universe.

- Indecision is the key to flexibility.

- I used to be indecisive now I'm just not sure.

- Play fair.

These sayings give us some interesting insights into each personality type. Notice that the Promoter is relational, encouraging and self-effacing . . . very yellow Promoter. The Planner gives task-oriented advice and is quite no nonsense . . . very blue Planner. The Producer is performance oriented, direct, and blunt, sometimes mixed with sarcasm . . . very red Producer. The Peacekeeper champions harmony, self-examination, and independence . . . very green Peacekeeper.

So the final action strategy is: take the *Live, Laugh, Love* advice of the Promoter. Add in *Your word is your bond* character quality from the Planner. You've read this book and can now start to speak the language of other personality types. So the Producer is right: *A job well begun is half done.* Follow the Peacekeeper's *Golden Rule* and you will have a well-balanced approach to relationships.

# ACKNOWLEDGMENTS

Thanks to the encouragement and support of so many wonderful people in my life, this new book has come to fruition. Thank you to my husband Fred, who is my unofficial editor, main encourager, and sounding board; and my children and grandchildren whose lives I call upon for inspiration.

Under the category of, "What are friends for if you can't use their great talents?," I thank Dr. James Schmook and his wife Kay for brainstorming titles, subtitles, and cover ideas with me; Suzzi Marquis for the limericks and redrafting many awkward sections; Armeme Humber and Dr. Pat Rexroat Parsons who help me think out loud; Alyce Quackenbush for her artistic input and encouragement to "talk it, not write it"; Judy Kane and Marie Harper for giving me their wise opinions, Laurie Parton, for seeing the value in the concept and being a great encourager; my cheerleaders, who let me know in spoken and unspoken ways that they believe in me (you know who you are). Thank you to Wayne and Diane Tesch and Pete and Susan McKenzie, who speak the People Skills Series language so fluently that we can communicate without talking.

Thanks to all the People Skills Series certified trainers who gave me material, including stories, and editing advice. Special thank you to Laura Angotti, Michelle Carrington, Kathy Wenig, Sue Green, Alicia Economos, Becky Newman, Phil and

Barbara Pompineau, Bob Chonka, Teri Pearson, Julie Donaghy, Gary Johnson, Sam Lupica, and Ron Brenning; your input from working with audiences across the country is found in these pages. Thanks to Royal Family Kids for using the concepts found in this book to build teams that communicate with understanding and love as they minister to abused children in the foster care system.

Thank you to my publishing team, including my editor, Marly Cornell, who "got me" and added an immense amount of wisdom because we were immediately on the same page in our initial conversation; my graphic artist, Carl Spady, for keeping the branding on track—our long association made you adept at reading my mind.

Lastly, thanks to the rocks in my life, my Bible Study groups— for listening to me, believing in me, and praying for me. Thank you Wednesday Bible study, Influencers, and my St. James supporters led by Reverend Cathie Young. Your constant reminder, that all things are possible though God who gives me strength, has been the foundation and provided me with the energy to write once again about a topic I truly believe adds value to people's lives.

# ABOUT THE AUTHOR

Vicki Barnes is the author of *The Kid Book . . . Surprising Truths about the People We Call Kids* and the president of Vicki Barnes Seminars, a firm specializing in team building training, customer service, presentation/speech coaching and certification training for the People Skills Series. As a professional speaker and trainer, she has shared her expertise in relationship management and effective communications with corporations, nonprofits, and educational audiences around the world.

Barnes is a proud mother and grandmother. She and her husband Frederick live in Newport Beach, California, where she is a volunteer advocate and spokesperson for children living within the foster care system.

Please visit her website: www.peopleskills4u.com.

# NOTES

# NOTES

# NOTES